UNBEATABLE

Praise for the book

"There can be nothing more liberating than proving your mettle to yourself, and breaking your own boundaries. Sadly, our society often sees differently-abled people as less capable than others. So when someone breaks this presumption, through their words and actions, it makes life better for a larger set of people.

Tapasvi's determination in the face of all odds and the support his family gives out is exemplary. This book brings to us an inspiring story of dedication, hard work, unconditional love and their unbeatable spirit."

– *SHATABDI AWASTHI (Gold Medalist in Berlin World Grand Prix, International Para Athlete)*

"*Unbeatable* is Tapasvi's remarkable story which reinforces the power of unflinching determination. Whether you perceive something as an obstacle or a disguised opportunity, it is up to you to determine the course of your life. Nothing is impossible if you have the courage to break out of your shell and excel."

– *POOJA AGARWAL (Para shooter, Silver medal winner at World Shooting Para Sports World Cup, Peru)*

"Tapasvi and Ajay have proved that there can be no team better than family, more so a father-son duo. It is commendable how they have together crossed hurdles and faced all challenges that came their way.

Ajay is doing a great job in spreading more knowledge about Cerebral Palsy. After all, knowledge is the strongest tool to cut through a society working on judgments and presumptions.

This book is a treasure comprising an inspirational story and valuable anecdotes from medical professionals and special educators, among others."

– *YOGESH KHATUNIA (Silver medalist in Tokyo Paralympics)*

UNBEATABLE

Celebrating Life with Cerebral Palsy

SHIKHI SHARMA

Srishti
PUBLISHERS & DISTRIBUTORS

Srishti Publishers & Distributors
A unit of AJR Publishing LLP
212A, Peacock Lane
Shahpur Jat, New Delhi – 110 049
editorial@srishtipublishers.com

First published by
Srishti Publishers & Distributors in 2021

10 9 8 7 6 5 4 3 2 1

This is a work of non-fiction, based on the author's experiences and life-learnings. It takes into account a true story, which is retold here with due permission. The recommendations given herein are in no way intended to be a substitute for professional advice and help.

Printed and bound in India

For Tashvi,

The angel of my life.

"You can't skip chapters, that's not how life works. You have to read every line, meet every character. You won't enjoy all of it. Hell, some chapters will make you cry for weeks. You will read things you don't want to read, you will have moments when you don't want the pages to end. But you will have to keep going. Stories keep the world revolving. Live yours, don't miss out."

– Courtney Peppernell

Contents

Contents

Acknowledgement

I couldn't have written this book without the continuous encouragement and help I received from various people in my life. I owe a lot to these people and extend my heartfelt gratitude.

My parents, who inculcated in me the genes of writing.

My in-laws, for giving me the required atmosphere for writing.

My daughter Tashvi, who is my oxygen, the reason that I breathe.

Tarun, my husband, my life, my constant pillar of strength.

My sister Mansi, for being surer about me completing this book than I was.

My sisters-in-law, for their constant encouragement.

Dipti Patel, you have been like a blessing to me.

Arup, Stuti, Vini and the entire team of Srishti Publishers. Your level of patience and support is unmatched.

All my colleagues and friends within and outside my working space, you all have been a constant support.

Ajay and Manju Sharma, for welcoming me, not only into their home, but also into their lives.

Tapasvi, for sharing his deepest, darkest shortcomings with me.

Manasvi, whom I deeply admire. Now, I also respect you bro, for the incredible person you are.

All the doctors, specialists, teachers and parents who took out time for this book and shared their thoughts and knowledge on this subject.

To my extended maternal and paternal family for their support.

Divyansh, for all his weird but fruitful ideas.

Lastly, my paternal and maternal grandfathers, for guiding me from the heavens above.

Prologue

The bougainvillea glowed bright pink in the mid-day sunlight, light rays flickering on and off the tender petals with the flow of the wind.

Winters in Jaipur have a way of making their presence felt, entering the city with hues and softness of pink, thereby creating an atmosphere of optimism and hope. The vibe of the city becomes sprightlier with warm aromas drifting within the city. The traces of cold weather can be felt in the mannerisms of the city, the tea stalls emanating tempting aromas, natives in variegated sweaters huddling near those stalls, and the early risers giving food to birds near Albert Hall.

And here I am, sitting in the cosy cocoon of one of the gazetted officers of Jaipur on a sunny day. Mr Ajay

Prologue

Sharma is ecstatic; his son Tapasvi has just cleared his NET[1] examination.

The drawing room is colossal, with a glistening chandelier adorning the middle of room. A Buddha mural near the entrance emits good vibes for all and sundry. The bougainvillea is clearly visible from the tall windows, reflecting the rays of the sun casting a warm glow over the opposite walls. I could feel the same warmth and happiness in Mr Ajay's eyes.

"You see," he mutters while taking a sip of hot tea and pouring some more from the blue pottery kettle into my cup. "The feat is not a small one. It is indeed Tapasvi's hard work and persistence that has earned him this accolade today. His incredible journey of twenty-two years was filled with challenges, but he didn't give up. There were moments when I wanted to back out, but he didn't. He stood strong with unfaltering courage in the face of adversities. There have been moments when we wanted to switch grounds, but Tapasvi endured everything. The outcome is for you to see."

I felt a bit sceptical about this description.

"Mr Ajay," I said, after listening to everything intently. "Indeed clearing NET is a great achievement, perhaps a dream for many. But, what did you mean when you said 'incredible journey of twenty-two years was filled with challenges'. Surely, he didn't start struggling the day he was born."

---

1. National Eligibility Test.

Ajay took a brief pause. Instead of speaking, he called Tapasvi to the living room. We had been waiting for a while before Tapasvi finally entered the room. One look at him melted away all my doubts.

Tapasvi had not just beaten this challenging entrance exam, but also Cerebral Palsy.

▼

"Hello ma'am!" The moment Tapasvi spoke, I understood why Mr Ajay was so proud of his child.

With a shaky, yet confident voice, crutches that held him upright and a slightly stiff demeanour, Tapasvi didn't look like a fragile figure at all. His eyes radiated a lot of power and determination which, I believe, was a driving force behind his success. His hunger for achieving great heights of excellence was clearly fathomable.

Sensing my uneasiness, he said, "Don't feel bad, ma'am. I am absolutely fine. In fact, I am euphoric right now, after my result. I have finally accomplished my dream. And I am really excited to share the news of my selection in my friends-circle. Seeya later!" With that, Tapasvi moved out of the room.

A boy, who looked very similar to Tapasvi, helped him walk out. I was a bit perplexed as I could only see his face partially.

Judging my expression, Mr Ajay added, "He is Tapasvi's twin brother, Manasvi."

After what I had seen, I had only one question to ask. "Do you have time for one more cup of tea?"

1

An Unexpected Beginning

God gives responsibilities to those who have the ability to fulfil them. I feel I am one of those blessed ones.

Twenty-two years ago, our life took a beautiful turn when my wife Manju discovered that she was expecting. I vividly remember the day that changed our lives forever.

Manju broke the news to me the moment I returned from office. I worked in the legal department of the Government of Rajasthan and Manju was a government teacher. We had a very simple life, until that fateful day. The news was a source of immense joy to us as we had earlier braved through one failed pregnancy. My parents became extra cautious as they wanted to ensure that Manju received the best care and support. We just couldn't take any chances this time around.

But one day, Manju had a slight accident and she started bleeding. When she was rushed to the hospital, we found out that Manju was going to have twins. We were so thrilled that we didn't pay heed to the doctor when she said that one child was showing some movement. Though the doctor did not say anything about the second child, in our excitement, we didn't even enquire.

The kids were due sometime in September and we started all the preparations at home. I carved out a small wooden crib for the children myself. But as they say, 'Man proposes, god disposes'. The babies decided to surprise us in July itself.

Completely unprepared, I rushed my wife to the hospital in the middle of the night. I did all I could to keep Manju in positive spirits, and she demonstrated a lot of strength throughout the ride, despite being in so much pain.

On 7 July, I got a glance of Tapasvi and Manasvi for the first time. They were born prematurely at seven-and-a-half months. With milk-white complexion, fuchsia lips, button nose and tiny fingers, Manasvi rolled his fingers around mine when I tried to touch him. However, Tapasvi could just palpate.

Little did I know that I would be coiling my finger around Tapasvi's for the rest of our lives.

Manasvi was doing fine, but for Tapasvi, the war had just begun. I speculated that it was because he cried a little late. I couldn't think of any other reason back then.

Manju and Manasvi were discharged on the third day itself, but Tapasvi was advised to be kept in the incubator for a week more. Those seven days were a glimpse into what lay ahead of us as a family.

After Tapasvi was discharged, a whole new set of rituals began to be followed in our family. Cleanliness became our primary concern and our house started smelling of phenyl and Dettol most of the time.

"Tapasvi is fragile. You will have to take care of him," the doctors and hospital staff advised us. We did not understand the weight of the word 'fragile' back then.

Honestly, having twins was a blessing. But it proved rather useful in another way also. It helped us identify Tapasvi's lapses. The presence of a twin brother helped us in comparing and identifying the progress of both my boys. Manasvi could be fed easily, while Tapasvi resisted. Manasvi could roll up the side, while Tapasvi couldn't. Manasvi used to respond to our smiles, but Tapasvi didn't. My mother also noticed the rigidity in Tapasvi's body while bathing the kids.

Since we all could see the differences clearly, we were prepared for some issue that could have become a part of Tapasvi's upbringing. I hadn't thought in my wildest dreams that it would give him an entirely different life.

2

Efforts to Know More

While we tried our best to give both the boys the best in everything, I didn't want Tapasvi to slacken in any way, no matter what the predicament was. I was ready to move mountains to support him through his physical complication.

I perceived it as a mere complication because the only assessment I received from the doctors about his categorical contortion was 'delayed milestone'. For the uninitiated, milestones are markers for a child's development, which help parents keep a tab on when a child must start doing a particular activity. These could be as small as smiling, emoting, turning on their stomach, to tougher ones like teething and \\walking.

Every doctor that I visited gave me a standard response. "You need not worry about anything, Mr Ajay. It is just a case of delayed milestones. Given the fact that he was a premature baby, it could just be his body taking time to recuperate. There is nothing wrong with your child."

Those explanations used to give me a ray of hope initially, but when I didn't see any improvement, I started becoming restless. I was looking for answers , which I could never find.

On a chilly November morning, I received some clarity amidst this darkness when Manju and I took Tapasvi to Dr Puri in GB Pant Hospital in Delhi. Tapasvi looked plump due to the numerous layers of woollens we made him wear to save him from the biting cold.

The doctor's chamber had white plastered walls and a giant wooden polished desk. The room had an overwhelming smell of Betadine which added to the typical hospital vibe of the place. I had visited countless hospitals by now, so the ambience was not new to me.

I began explaining Tapasvi's condition to the doctor. Even before I had finished, the doctor picked up Tapasvi from his torso and held him high. The moment he did that, Tapasvi's legs crossed, forming an X.

On the diagnosis slip, he wrote *Cerebral Palsy (spastic)* and referred us for occupational therapy the same day.

We were completely confused as we did not have even the slightest idea about cerebral palsy. How would we support our child through something about which we were not even aware!

It was during the occupational therapy session with the physiotherapist that we got a glimpse of the complexities of cerebral palsy.

The physiotherapist said, "There is no cure for cerebral palsy, but the intensity can be reduced by physiotherapy."

His words pierced my heart. His words 'no cure' kept echoing in my mind. I was stunned, unable to fathom what to do next.

The physiotherapist then referred us to the biggest private hospital of Jaipur at that time – Santokba Durlabhji Memorial Hospital.

Tapasvi was referred to Dr Nanawati and we consulted him as soon as we reached Jaipur. My first meeting with Dr Nanawati, his analysis of Tapasvi's medical condition and the first physiotherapy session made it evident that my life would not be the same ever again.

You must note that here, we are referring to a time when internet was not advanced and medical journals were not easily available. We struggled endlessly to educate ourselves on the subject of cerebral palsy to understand its intricacies. The more we read about it, the tougher it seemed to find a way through.

I wouldn't be lying if I say I wasn't crestfallen and doleful. The sword had struck more unfavourably than I had expected. Even before I could absorb the joy of having two lovely kids, my happiness was snatched away. I knew that my Tapasvi would never be able to enjoy a carefree life like other children.

Deep down, I also knew that this forlorn attitude would lead me nowhere. I had to be strong and develop a more solution-oriented approach to my circumstances. Before we could proceed further with the therapy, we had to accept our situation. As a family, we had to come together and face this as a team as it wasn't my solo journey. As Helen Keller rightly says, "Alone we can do so little, together we can do so much."

▼

When I was in sixth standard, my parents used to reside in Narnol, Haryana. I did my schooling from there. A girl used to live in our neighbourhood. Unlike other kids, she had a very different physiognomy. She was not in a shape we are so used to; her mouth used to drool, and her hair was unkempt and dreggy. She couldn't walk properly and her speech was discontinuous.

I didn't understand her condition back then. But, while the doctor was elaborating on cerebral palsy, the memory of that girl came flashing in my mind. I recollected all my brief interactions with her and analyzed them with a fresh perspective. My past experiences with her acted as a springboard to identify with Tapasvi's medical condition and support him better.

I had spent many hours dwelling on the word 'why', pondering deeply on various possibilities and self-doubts.

Why did it happen to my child? Why did I not know about it before? Could we have averted this? Why can it not be cured? Will I be able to give a good life to my child?

But, I resolved to change my perspective and embrace my circumstances. It was only then that my question changed from "why" to "how".

What is Cerebral Palsy?

Back when we needed more information on Cerebral Palsy, we had to struggle, due to the lack of easily available information and resources. Here's a description from the experts which will help you understand cerebral palsy and its symptoms better.

The words '*cerebral*' and '*palsy*' refer to impairment of motor function. Cerebral palsy, therefore, is a group of neurological disorders affecting body movement and muscle coordination in infants or young children. It is caused by abnormalities during foetal growth or injuries before, during, or after birth.

Cerebral palsy (CP) affects the brain's cerebral cortex region (motor area) that is responsible for directing muscle movement. It interrupts the brain's development process, causing difficulty in controlling movements or maintaining balance.

Some identifiable symptoms of CP in children include:

- Ataxia - the lack of muscle coordination during voluntary movements
- Spasticity - contraction or stiffness of muscles for a prolonged time
- Feeble arm(s) or leg(s)
- Walking on the toes, a crouched gait, or a 'scissored' gait
- Alterations between stiff or floppy muscle tone
- Swallowing, speaking or drooling difficulties
- Experiencing random involuntary movements or tremors
- Slow development of fine motor skills
- Struggling with precision, such as writing or buttoning a shirt.

While CP is permanent, the symptoms are not. They may fluctuate over time, and their extent is different among different people, depending on the area of the injury.

Difficulty in moving and maintaining a posture are the most common symptoms of people diagnosed with CP. Some individuals also experience intellectual disability, seizures and abnormal physical sensations or perceptions, impaired vision or hearing, language and speech problems and other medical disorders.

The effect of CP isn't always extreme, but it still remains one of the dominant causes of childhood disabilities. A child with a lesser impact of CP might not show any signs of the disorder except for slight awkwardness. On the other hand, a child profoundly affected by CP may require special attention, extensive care and external support to walk. The degree of the existing symptoms could become more or less distinct with age, but the disorder itself isn't progressive.

Cerebral palsy affects 3.3 children per 1,000 live births, according to a study conducted by the Centers for Disease Control and Prevention (CDC). Unfortunately, CP is not a curable disorder, but some treatments, medications and surgeries help with developing the child's motor and communication skills.

What are the early signs?

Symptoms of cerebral palsy appear in infants, but an accurate diagnosis is possible only after the child completes two years of age. A delay in the child's ability to roll over, sit, crawl, walk, or other such developmental issues hint towards CP. Yet another indication of CP is an abnormal muscle tone, which could either be hypotonia (child appears relaxed or floppy) or hypertonia (child appears stiff or rigid).

Possibly, hypotonia could also progress to hypertonia after the child turns two or three months old. Some children suffering from CP may demonstrate abnormal postures or lean more towards one side of their body when they reach for something, move or crawl, although some children demonstrate similar behaviour even when they don't have CP. Parents should therefore avoid self-diagnosis on the basis of general information until diagnosed by a medical professional.

Some early warning signs are as follows:

Babies younger than six months could show the following signs:

- A lagging head when lifted from sleeping position

- Stiffness
- Floppiness
- Crossing or scissoring of legs when picked up

Babies over six months of age could show the following signs:

- Not rolling in any direction
- Trouble bringing hands together
- Difficulty bringing hands to the mouth
- Fisting one hand and reaching out with the other

Babies over ten months of age could show the following signs:

- Lopsided crawling - exerting only one hand and leg while dropping the opposite hand and leg
- Inability to stand using support

What causes Cerebral Palsy?

As indicated, abnormal development, problems with blood flow to the brain, head injury from a motor vehicle accident, child abuse, or infections such as bacterial meningitis or viral encephalitis in the motor area of the brain could lead to cerebral palsy. Studies indicate that a large group of children diagnosed with CP have *congenital cerebral palsy* (that is, they were born with it). Doctors cannot identify the disorder until the child is a few months or a year old.

- **Damage to the white matter of the brain (*periventricular leukomalacia*, or PVL)**

The brain's white matter carries out the function of transmitting messages to the rest of the body. But damage from PVL that looks like tiny holes or gaps interferes with this function. Factually, a foetal brain requires twenty-six to thirty-four weeks for development, also called the gestation period. During this phase, the PVL is delicate and susceptible to injuries.

- **Cerebral Dysgenesis - Abnormal development of the brain**

Brain malformations caused by disruptions in a foetus' development restrict the transmission of brain signals. Mutations in the genes could affect the normal development of the brain. Conditions such as infections, fevers, trauma, etc., are risky for the foetus' nervous system owing to the womb's ill health.

- **Intracranial Haemorrhage - Bleeding in the brain**

Blocked or broken blood vessels because of a foetal stroke cause a brain bleed. Blood clots in the placenta or an interruption in the blood's flow to the brain when a baby is in a womb is the main trigger for a stroke. Abnormal or weak blood vessels, hypertension during pregnancy, and maternal infection such as pelvic inflammatory diseases are other reasons for foetal strokes, leading to bleeding in the brain.

- **Asphyxia - Severe lack of oxygen in the brain**

Stress or breathing difficulties during labour pains or delivery could cut off or interrupt the flow of oxygen to the brain. Although a baby can handle it for a short period, but a shortage of oxygen in the brain for an extended time leads to *hypoxic-ischemic encephalopathy,* a type of brain damage.

In this condition, the tissues in the cerebral motor cortex and other areas of the brain are destroyed. Unusually low blood pressure during pregnancy, a rupture in the uterus, detachment of the placenta, complications in the umbilical cord, trauma or head injury during labour or delivery could also lead to a similar kind of damage.

What are the risk factors?

Certain pregnancy and delivery-related medical conditions put the unborn baby at the greatest risk of cerebral palsy post-birth. Some such risks include:

- *Low birth weight and premature birth*: Babies born during their gestational period are at extreme risk for CP. A full-term baby born with the required weight runs a lower risk of CP as opposed to premature babies born less than thirty-seven weeks into pregnancy or weighing less than 5 ½ pounds.
- *Multiple births*: Fully developed babies born as twins, triplets, or in other multiple birth scenarios are more prone to cerebral palsy. In case one of those babies dies, those alive are at a greater risk.
- *Infections during pregnancy:* Contracting infections like toxoplasmosis, rubella (German measles), cytomegalovirus, and herpes during pregnancy could also lead to an infection in the womb and placenta. Such inflammations have a detrimental effect on an unborn baby's nervous system, thus increasing the risk of being born with CP. Experiencing maternal fever during pregnancy or childbirth could also lead to similar damaging inflammations.

- *Blood type incompatibility between mother and child:* Rh incompatibility is one of the high-risk causes for cerebral palsy. It refers to the condition when the baby and mother's Rh blood type (positive or negative) are dissimilar. In such cases, the mother's body creates antibodies to fight and attack the presence of another blood type, killing the foetus's blood cells, ultimately leading to brain damage.
- *Exposure to toxic substances:* Exposure to toxic substances like methyl mercury during pregnancy endangers the baby with cerebral palsy.
- *Thyroid abnormalities, intellectual disability, excess protein in the urine, or seizures:* Any of these conditions in expecting mothers could be the cause of CP in the child.

During labour, delivery and post-delivery, a mother could experience some medical conditions that could also indicate cerebral palsy in the child, but the chances of the child developing CP are low.

Breech presentation - A breech position refers to the condition in which a baby's feet crown before the head during labour. Babies with CP or floppy babies are mostly in a breech presentation during labour.

Complicated labour and delivery - The signs of vascular or respiratory issues during labour or delivery could indicate brain damage or abnormalities.

Small for their gestational age - Factors interfering with a baby's natural growth in the womb could risk the baby from being born smaller than other children in that gestational age. They are likely to be diagnosed with CP later.

Low Apgar score - A newborn baby's heart rate, breathing, muscle tone, reflexes, and skin colour require immediate monitoring after birth and then again around twenty minutes later. Doctors score the baby based on these readings. If the score remains low even after twenty minutes, it refers to a low Apgar score, a rating scale to analyze the infant's health, which could be a vital indicator of cerebral palsy.

Jaundice - The occurrence of jaundice in newborns is common. More than fifty percent of babies develop jaundice indicated by the yellowing of the skin and the sclera (the white part of the eyes) after birth. Jaundice typically means the fast-paced building of bilirubin, a substance found in the bile juice, making it difficult for the liver to break it down. If jaundice doesn't come down at the required rate of healing or remains untreated, it damages the brain cells, and could lead to deafness and CP.

Seizures - Seizures are warning signals of the possibility of the infant developing cerebral palsy as a child.

What are the different forms of cerebral palsy?

The degree, kind and exact place of abnormality in a child's brain define the different forms of cerebral palsy. Typically, doctors identify the type based on movement disorder. Which means that they classify CP according to the type of movement disorder involved.

Based on this classification, the different forms of CP include – Spastic (stiff muscles), athetoid (writhing movements), or ataxic (poor balance and coordination), along with other symptoms like paresis (weakness) or plegia (paralysis).

To elucidate, hemiparesis (hemi means half) and Quadriplegia (quad means four) specifies that only half of all four limbs are being affected, respectively. The most common form of cerebral palsy is Spastic cerebral palsy that refers to tight muscles and uncoordinated movement.

What other conditions are associated with cerebral palsy?

Intellectual disability - One of the most common conditions associated with cerebral palsy is intellectual disability, affecting between 35% of people diagnosed with CP. As already understood, it is spastic quadriplegia that has the most drastic effect causing mental impairment than the other forms of CP.

Seizure disorder - Most types of cerebral palsy are accompanied by different kinds of seizures. Half the children with CP suffer from varying seizure types. Children diagnosed with both CP and epilepsy run a higher risk of intellectual disability.

Delayed growth and development - Cerebral palsy directly impacts a child's growth and development process, especially in cases of spastic quadriparesis. A below-average weight gain in babies is an example of delayed development in babies. Children who are supposed to be a little older can be abnormally short, much like teenagers, who could also lack sexual development.

On the other hand, children with spastic hemiplegia could experience muscle problems. Their limbs in the affected area see prolonged growth in comparison to the other limb.

Spinal deformities and osteoarthritis: Some irregularities associated with CP include scoliosis (curvature of the spine), kyphosis (a humpback), and lordosis (a saddleback).

The spine supports the body in performing almost all basic body functions like sitting, standing and walking. But the chronic pain that comes with such spinal deformities in CP makes it difficult to do any of these with ease. In some cases, there is a chance of osteoporosis in individuals with CP, a condition in which the joint's cartilages break and the bone enlarges. Excessive pressure on joints or their misalignment is the root cause of osteoporosis.

Impaired vision - Strabismus is yet another associated condition of CP, which people otherwise identify as 'cross eyes'. The major drawback of not treating strabismus could either be deteriorating vision in one eye or reduced spatial abilities. The extent of impaired vision differs in children. While some children with CP cannot fathom visual information like that of graphic art, still photography, moving photography, etc., some others could suffer from more drastic vision defects like visual impairment or blurriness in both eyes or one eye.

Hearing loss - CP doesn't just interfere with normal visual functions, but also with hearing functions in several children. There is more than one reason for this kind of impaired hearing, but two general reasons include being infected with jaundice or reduced oxygen supply to an infant's brain. This loss could either be partial or complete.

Speech and language disorders - Almost one-third population of people suffering from CP sustains cognitive impairment. Such people cannot form or say words with clarity. Impaired speech is one of those effects associated with CP that doesn't just deprive the child of having normal communication skills, but also eventually frustrates them. This kind of extremity usually occurs in children with average or above-average intelligence.

Drooling - Children or adults diagnosed with CP don't have much control over their throat, mouth and tongue muscles. Drooling, therefore, becomes an associated condition for them.

Incontinence - Incontinence is the lack of self-restraint or control over the body's voluntary movements related to bladder control. Individuals with CP could develop incontinence, during which they lose control over the bladder muscles.

Abnormal sensations and perceptions - When it comes to sensations, CP could affect an individual in two ways – either they could feel extreme pain or not have any feeling of the primary sensations like that of touch.

Learning difficulties - Cerebral palsy is the result of brain damage in a certain area of the brain. A possible condition of CP includes a lack in the potential to process spatial or auditory information because of an injury on the area that controls the development and functioning of language and intellectual abilities.

Infections and long-term illnesses - It is noticed that adults with CP are more prone to heart and lung diseases like pneumonia (often from inhaling bits of food into the lungs) than those without the disorder.

Contractures - One of the other painful effects of CP is contractures, a condition in which muscles deform and take abnormal positions. Besides being painful, they are also the cause of muscle spasticity and joint deformities.

Malnutrition - As commonly understood, CP develops very early on in an individual's life, typically during infancy. It is a phase when babies require ample nutrition and maintenance of their weight. But the condition of cerebral palsy makes swallowing, sucking or feeding strenuous, thus leading to malnutrition.

Dental problems - Among the many other conditions associated with CP are dental problems like gum diseases and cavities. The cause of this could either be improper dental hygiene or medications that worsen this situation. Commonly, the drugs prescribed to treat seizures aggravate dental problems in children with cerebral palsy.

Inactivity - Cerebral palsy is sourced from damage to the area of the brain that controls the body's motor and voluntary movements. Children with CP necessitate more energy in daily functions like walking, playing, etc., making them more inactive over time. With age, the severity of inactivity worsens, deteriorating the overall health and wellness of an individual.

How is cerebral palsy diagnosed?

Even though cerebral palsy forms when in the womb, during, or after birth, diagnosing it is not possible until the child turns two. In those cases when the symptoms aren't distinct or are mild, medical practitioners cannot draw a confirmed diagnosis until the child turns four or five. Any diagnosis before this age in children with mild symptoms cannot be confirmed or reliable.

The medical procedure to diagnose CP is based on a chain of tests that assess the child's motor skills. Doctors who detect signs or symptoms of CP observe the child's development, growth, muscle tone, age-appropriate motor control, hearing and vision, posture and coordination, during all regular check-ups for two years (or more in case of mild symptoms).

During these years, the doctor rules out all other diseases with similar symptoms as CP. A significant factor to monitor is that the problems shouldn't advance as cerebral palsy is not a progressive disorder. However, the symptoms could alter. For example, a gradual loss of motor skills could hint towards other disorders or diseases such as genetic or muscle disease, metabolism disorder, or tumours in the nervous system.

Diagnosing CP with accuracy demands lab tests that study other possible disorders with symptoms similar to as CP.

Much like these metabolic disorders, though, several other disorders could either trigger a type of CP or could be misunderstood as CP.

An example of such a disorder is coagulation disorders, a condition of preventing blood clots or causing excessive clotting, leading to strokes before or after birth. The symptoms of coagulation disorder and CP are almost the same, mostly bending towards a diagnosis of hemiparetic CP.

Doctors dealing with such cases then refer to specialists such as a child neurologist, developmental paediatrician, ophthalmologist or oncologist, who together reach towards accuracy in the diagnosis. These specialists also work on developing a treatment plan for such individuals.

Is cerebral palsy preventable?

According to medical findings, cerebral palsy is an unpreventable genetic abnormality. However, science offers some relief to women who are looking forward to reducing, managing or avoiding the risk factors for congenital cerebral palsy.

Vaccinating against diseases like the German measles, also called rubella, is one such helpful way. During early pregnancy, it is possible to stabilize Rh incompatibilities to evade future risks. The use of car seats could also prevent acquired cerebral palsy in young children.

3

Tapasvi's Physiotherapy Sessions

With whatever little knowledge we were equipped with till then, we knew that we couldn't intermit Tapasvi's physiotherapy at any cost. So we took Tapasvi to Dr Nanawati for the first time on 3 December 1998.

Whenever I recall the mushrooming years of my son's life, I still feel the warm soft sun rays filtering through this bougainvillea plant, casting a shadow on the opposite wall in the late evenings. The aroma of cardamom and the cosy fleece that I would wrap around the children are deeply etched in my mind. The winter season is, after all, integral to the important epochs of Tapasvi's life.

Dr Nanawati was clear and straightforward in her approach towards cerebral palsy. She bluntly told me, "Physiotherapy won't cure cerebral palsy; it can only abate its magnitude. But at the same time, if there is anything that can help Tapasvi, it's physiotherapy."

The point was loud and clear. We sought advice from her and started off with trying to help Tapasvi learn how to turn in bed. The process involved holding a bed sheet from corners and rolling him inside it slowly to make him understand how he could turn on his side. It might seem to be a very simple task, but it took us six months to teach him this. When we saw him executing it on his own, it was a moment to behold for us. That small accomplishment paved way for bigger ones.

When I look back, I realise how Tapasvi made me mature as a person; he helped me grow. I learned the virtue of patience. He had to be coached for the smallest of things, like holding his head as he couldn't balance his neck. He had to be taught how to hold something in his fingers as he didn't have the grip. We taught him things like how to stop his drooling, how to hold the spoon and every little movement you can imagine. It was never cake walk because it took us a couple of months to achieve effective results.

The bi-monthly visits to Dr Nanawati continued for two years. We never missed a single appointment. I did not have the luxury of falling ill, because there was always a question looming over my head – "What if".

The passage from the archway of Santokba Durlabhji hospital till Dr Nanawati's chamber is still fresh in my mind –

the giant yellow hospital located in a prime zone, the smell of Betadine always lingering around and the big glass walls that gave a glimpse of the greenery around the hospital premises.

The doctor executed a set of tasks on every visit – she would first perform varied exercises on Tapasvi and then ask us to repeat the same in front of her to ensure that we were doing it correctly. We had to do the same exercises for two weeks before visiting the hospital again. Whatever she said was like a word of god for me. She was my only hope, the only discernible source of Tapasvi's recuperation.

Unlike what we presume these days, physiotherapy was a rather painful process – physically for Tapasvi and mentally for me. Tapasvi used to feel excruciating pain in his body during the process of physiotherapy.

Imagine an infant who has not yet celebrated his first birthday, going through such a harrowing process. He was too young to even fathom the reason why this pain was being rendered on his body. His screams and wails from the physiotherapy room haunt me even today. Even when I used to repeat those exercises at home with Tapasvi, I used to close the door. I didn't want my family to witness Tapasvi's painful plight.

During our fourth session with Dr Nanawati, when I had stepped out of the physiotherapy room, carrying a sobbing Tapasvi in my arms, I met Dr Omkar, one of the paediatricians at the hospital. Dr Omkar's son, who was just a year older than Tapasvi, had also been diagnosed with the same medical condition. He had a better insight about doctors in Jaipur who were engaged in analysis and cure of cerebral palsy.

I had tried numerous avenues, but was still struggling to decipher much information about the treatment of cerebral palsy. Which is why it felt like Dr Omkar had come into our lives as a blessing in disguise.

"Mr Sharma," he said, "our patients fill us with hope. Believe me! Being a paediatrician, I have seen the discomfort and ordeal of children in certain conditions. The parents have a lot of power to support their child with a lot of hope. Their prayers often make miracles happen. Their mindset transforms adversities into opportunities."

With those words, he left for his chamber. His words reignited my hopes and spirits.

The second time I met him, Dr Omkar recommended a visit to Dr Sunil Gupta, who had conducted a research on cerebral palsy. I took Tapasvi to Dr Sunil, hoping to receive quality guidance.

After talking with Dr Sunil, a new set of treatment followed. Tapasvi used to start his day with exercises prescribed by Dr Nanawati, following it up with the medicines prescribed by Dr Sunil. This continued for five years.

It was arduous, since both my wife and I were working. We also had to look after Manasvi, as we wanted to give him adequate attention. As a family, we used to have bouts of frustration, but we did not falter or lose sight of our goal. We followed the powerful mantra, 'this too shall pass, and the tide will turn around'.

In those five years, we were asked to assemble an hourly chart of Tapasvi's daily enterprises – How does he sleep? Does he ask for a specific toy? What kind of food does he prefer to eat?

A test called Single-photon emission computerized tomography (SPECT) was also advised to check the profusion of blood in the brain. It was an expensive test, but it was the least we could do when it came to our child's future. It was all premeditated as an investment in Tapasvi's future.

Once transacted, after a year of treatment, there was a slight boost in the blood profusion in the cerebrum area, but it wasn't satisfactory. I wanted to see some palpable development. I wanted to see my son move around like other kids. Tapasvi never repelled from trying new exercises or undergoing any surgery or a change in medication. Although he was too young then, I discerned that he was very resilient. No matter how much pain he might be experiencing, he never shared it with anyone.

Once during our physiotherapy sessions, Dr Nanawati advised us to go for hamstring's operation. If you're wondering why this wasn't suggested earlier, we should take note that cerebral palsy, as a medical condition, doesn't have a certain course of action. There was no specific set of steps that we had to undertake to achieve our purpose. It was all a hit and trial.

I decided to proceed further with the operation, in the anticipation of seeing some conclusive results. When I took an appointment to meet Dr Omkar, he didn't admonish us against the operation directly, but cautioned us that Dr Sunil Gupta would be strictly against it. When I approached Dr Sunil regarding my preference for the operation, he staunchly opposed my decision and kept my file at the corner of his desk.

By that stage, even I had become a bit embittered. We were not even close to a progressive outcome. I spent many nights trying to figure out ingenious ways get positive results. I tried everything that was possible. I even dug up a hole in the vacant neighbourhood plot and put Tapasvi in it, the sand reaching till his shoulders. I was hopeful that it would help in straightening his legs. I left him in midst of chickens to make him move, but nothing worked.

For the hamstring's operation, we approached the most acclaimed doctor of Jaipur, Dr PK Sethi. He had co-invented the Jaipur foot[1] and won Magsaysay Award and Padma Shree in 1981. I had heard many success stories of Dr PK Sethi's treatment. The operation was meant to lengthen the hamstring muscles to bolster Tapasvi in walking. While walking comes to us all rather naturally, it was a strenuous procedure for Tapasvi. It left him drained of all energy. The ectomorphic state of Tapasvi's body also proved to be a hindrance.

The surgery was a tormenting process with Tapasvi being in deep pain. The moment he gained consciousness and the effect of anaesthesia wore off, the hospital corridors were filled with his deep cries of physical pain and convalescence.

I remember Manju, my wife, holding back her tears. She asked if the pain was worth it. It was a very well lit room in which

---

1. a rubber-based prosthetic leg from below the knee.

Tapasvi was taken after the operation, sunlight reflecting from the metal hinges to which Tapasvi's legs were tied. Unfortunately, we were informed that the operation didn't yield the desired results.

There it was, my child in front of me, in the glistening, bright sunlight filled ward, unable to communicate because of muscular cramps. And I stood in front of him, unable to think clearly. A feeling of guilt engulfed me. We had again reached a dead end from where I could see no way out.

While I was disenchanted, I never thought of giving up. I was mindful of conditions such as deafness, Down syndrome and leprosy, but in those days, not much was known about cerebral palsy which is why, it was speculated to be a fruit of past misdeed.

I was appalled to see how we were treated differently at social gatherings, and even asked insensitive questions. Just the thought that if such words could hurt us so much, what would they do to Tapasvi made us change our outlook. Moreover, these toxic experiences never discouraged me from following my pursuit of building a better future for Tapasvi.

I knocked Dr Sunil's door again and again, but he refused to see us. He seemed to have felt offended because we had gone ahead with the surgery against his advice. However, I didn't give up. Finally when I persisted and showed up for the third time, he accepted our request and Tapasvi's treatment started again.

We heard about botox and how it could help in softening Tapasvi's muscles. I didn't think twice before proceeding with it.

We got his botox operation done. For a long duration after the operation, his legs were hung in a straight line upwards.

Once the surgery was over and his legs healed, Tapasvi could stretch his legs better. Our spirits were elevated with this small development, but it came with a clause!

We had to exercise his legs for eight hours continuously. As Tapasvi would say, "They stretched my legs like a rubber band."

The effect of botox wore off at a slow pace, so we had to exploit it to the fullest. As soon as the effect of botox withered away, his muscles became stiff again. It felt as if all the pain that he had endured was washed away with a strong wave.

I didn't get desirable results but I was not ready to quit. It was going to be a difficult battle and I rose to the challenge.

How is Cerebral Palsy Treated?

Since a solution-oriented approach helps fight such situations, let's read what the experts believe to be the right line of treatment for Cerebral Palsy.

Unfortunately, there is no permanent cure for cerebral palsy. Neither does the disorder progress, nor does it deteriorate. But some treatment methods help a child cope with the disorder and explore their capabilities in this condition. When children with CP receive the necessary treatment, they develop the potential to manage their condition better.

To attain the maximum benefit of these treatments, doctors immediately suggest one or more of these treatments soon after diagnosing CP. It helps children overcome, accept and cope with their condition sooner, giving them the hope and scope to pick up ways to wage through their daily lives. Such children also learn new and varying methods to accomplish challenging tasks.

The therapies available to treat CP differ from person to person. No two people with cerebral palsy are eligible for the same standard treatment therapy. Doctors first confirm the diagnosis after ruling out all other disorders. With the help of neuroimaging technique, they will then identify the type of CP. The doctor, his team and the parents then jointly observe the impairments in the child. In the final stage of beginning this therapy, the doctor works out a plan to deal with the child's impairments and creates a therapy plan to improve the child's quality of life.

- **Physical therapy -** Physical therapy is the foundation method for treating cerebral palsy. Doctors commence physical therapy soon after the diagnosis, prescribing specific exercises (such as resistive or strength training programs). This therapy also involves the child in prescribed activities to boost and maintain the child's muscle strength, balance and motor skills and prevent contractures. Children with mobility issues also receive special braces (called orthotic devices) to help improve mobility and stretching spastic muscles.
- **Occupational therapy -** Children with issues in their upper body functions and mobility usually undergo occupational therapy. This treatment optimizes the body's function, improvises posture issues and helps the child cope with daily activities. During occupation therapy, children learn

how to dress up, participate in other children's activities, go to school, etc., with their condition.

- **Recreation therapy** - Difficulty in mobility could make a child with CP inactive. Treatment with recreation therapy teaches children to participate in sports, cultural events and other art activities. Recreation therapy expands a child's physical and cognitive skills. Several parents of children diagnosed with CP reported a gradual improvement in their child's speech, self-esteem and emotional well-being through this therapy.
- **Speech and language therapy** - As the name suggests, this therapy works on a child's speech to improve clarity, overcome swallowing disorders and teach communication methods like sign language and special communication devices like a computer with a voice synthesizer. During speech and language therapy, therapists also present a special board of symbols to children with CP to help them point towards symbols to help them convey what they otherwise cannot.
- **Treatments for problems with eating and drooling** - CP affects children with eating and drinking processes due to lack of control over mouth, jaw and tongue muscles, leading to drooling. Children who experience eating problems with CP could breathe food or other fluids into their lungs, contract lung infections frequently and suffer from progressive lung diseases or malnutrition.

Drug Treatments

The treatment of cerebral palsy symptoms begins with prescribing oral medications that help in relaxing stiff, contracted or overactive muscles. These prescribed drugs are usually heavy and come with side effects like drowsiness, changes in blood pressure and the risk of liver damage. Doctors and caretakers monitor these to take immediate action in case of a reaction. Not all children with CP are prescribed these oral medications as they mostly work for those who require mild alteration in the muscle tone or for those with widespread spasticity.

- ***Botulinum toxin* (BT-A)** - One of the most standard treatments for overactive muscles in children with CP, BT-A is a drug locally injected into the body. The drug actively keeps the nerve cells from over-activating the muscle, thus reducing the stiffness in contracted muscles. Some side effects of this drug are pain in the injection area or mild flu. Neither of these is severe, though. The positive outcome of BT-A lasts for up to three months. Doctors recommend a stretching program that includes a few physical therapy sessions and splinting after injecting this drug to individuals. Although not every child with CT is eligible for BT-A as these drugs are most effective when there are only a limited number of flexible or unfixed muscles to treat. Basically, the child should not have total uncontrolled motor movements.
- ***Intrathecal baclofen*** - is a lot different from injecting BT-A. This therapy is a more complex procedure in which

an injectable pump carries a muscle relaxant to the spinal cord and injects it into the fluid that surrounds and protects the spinal cord. Sensitive nerve cells present in the spinal cord cause muscle spasticity in the body. This drug works on minimizing this sensitivity to ease muscle spasticity throughout the body. Doctors recommend this treatment for those individuals with CP who suffer from chronic, severe stiffness or uncontrolled muscle movement throughout the body.

Surgery

Individuals coping with severe stiffness or spasticity that interferes with basic movements like walking or moving could experience immense pain. An orthopedic surgery often comes as help, wherein doctors work on improving an individual's walk or posture. Such surgeries also help people with spinal deformities. One orthopedic procedure to treat CP includes tendon surgery, in which surgeons can increase the length of muscles and tendons, easing severe pain and making mobility less difficult. Not every child with CP can undergo orthopedic surgery, and the decision depends on the kind and extent of the symptoms. Surgeons decide these procedures at a time when they find it most appropriate. They also perform a quantitative gait analysis before deciding upon a surgical procedure when treating gait abnormalities.

Surgery to cut nerves - When all other treatment options – namely, physical therapy, oral medications, and intrathecal baclofen – fail to compose pain, doctors are left with no other option but to perform a Selective Dorsal Rhizotomy (SDR) to treat severe spasticity. SDR is a procedure to locate overactivated nerves and carefully sever them. This surgery relaxes stiff muscles, consequently relieving the individual from chronic pain usually felt in either or both legs. SDR is also performed in individuals with an overactive bladder. Sensory loss, numbness, or uncomfortable sensations in limb areas are some possible side effects of this surgical procedure.

Assistive devices

Individuals with cerebral palsy often suffer from a lack of communication abilities. But assistive devices like computers, computer software, voice synthesizers and picture books installed at home, workplaces or schools can help them communicate and independently carry on with day-to-day activities.

To make individuals with CP more self-sufficient with their mobility and offer them external support for muscle imbalance, doctors recommend the use of orthotic devices. Braces and splints are examples of such devices that tackle muscle abnormalities by making routine functions like walking or sitting less exhausting. Besides braces, wedges and special chairs are some other devices that work on stretching muscles, positioning joints and performing daily functions. Mobility issues sourced from CP require wheelchairs, rolling walkers and powered scooters to make such individuals move around with less support.

Glasses, magnifiers, large-print books, and computer typefaces are offered to individuals that require visual aids, but some extreme cases also undergo surgery to fix vision problems. Hearing difficulties can also be eased with the help of devices like hearing aids and telephone amplifiers.

Complementary and Alternative Therapies

There is also an availability of complementary or alternative medicines for children and adolescents with cerebral palsy. Mainstream clinical practice does not involve many of these therapies as a treatment for CP as they did not offer any conclusive or benefitting results when tested with controlled clinical trials.

A few subjective reports, on the contrary, reveal quite the opposite, claiming that these therapies have a positive impact. Although this treatment remains unapproved by the U.S. Food and Drug Administration, therapies like hyperbaric oxygen therapy, special clothing worn during resistance exercise training, certain forms of electrical stimulation, assisting children in completing certain motions several times a day, and specialized learning strategies are some such treatments. Responsible associations always warn parents of children with CP to check with their doctor before placing the child with any therapy, as the dietary supplements or herbal medicines provided with these officially unapproved therapies could react with the other drugs.

Researchers are also studying the effect of stem cell therapy as a treatment for cerebral palsy. Still at a premature stage of testing, it will be a while till they can find the desired results, safety concerns, and effect of this therapy. There is hope that stem cell therapy will become one of the revolutionizing therapies to repair damaged nerves and brain tissues as stem cells have the characteristics to take the form of other cells in the body. Presently, scientists in the US are studying the impact of infusing stem cells of the umbilical cord in CP children.

Are there treatments for other conditions associated with cerebral palsy?

Epilepsy - Epilepsy is common in several children who have both, intellectual disability and CP. Sadly, no specific drug helps treat intellectual disability, CP and epilepsy seizures simultaneously. Doctors prescribe medicines after examining the type of seizures, which sometimes also include combination drugs to achieve better results in controlling seizures.

Incontinence - There are some effective treatment options like special exercises, biofeedback, prescription drugs, surgery, or surgically implanted devices to treat the issue of incontinence.

Osteopenia - The lack of mobility in children with difficulty in walking is prone to osteopenia, a condition of weak bone density that ultimately results in broken bones.

National Institutes of Health (NIH) funded some older Americans to study the effect of *bisphosphonates*, an FDA-approved group of drugs. Commonly, these drugs are prescribed to elderly people suffering from low mineral density. This study indicated that these drugs also boost weak bone mineral density problems. Some doctors prescribe these off-label drugs to children with CP to avert the condition of osteopenia.

Pain - Spastic muscles and a strain on the body because of muscle abnormalities cause severe pain in individuals with CP. In some cases, the situation becomes extreme with frequent and unpredicted muscle spasms. Certain drugs have proven effective in lessening pain caused by muscle spasms and reducing the occurrence of painful spasms. Distraction, relaxation training, biofeedback, and therapeutic massages are advantageous, non-invasive, and drug-free remedies to control pain in adults and older children.

What Medical Experts Have to Say

Dr Sunil Kumar Gupta
MBBS, MD, PHD
Krishna Ram Hospital and Research Centre
Jaipur

When Mr Ajay called me up on a summery April evening, I couldn't recognise which patient of mine he was referring to.

'Tapasvi', the name struck a chord, but I couldn't place the details in my memory definitively.

I gave him an appointment for the next day and went about my business as usual. But there was a nagging feeling at the back of my head the whole day, about the boy named Tapasvi.

The next day, Mr Sharma was at my door at 5 p.m. sharp. He was quite shocked to see my deteriorating health after a span of around eighteen years, but didn't let it show on his face. He began the introduction and the face of a cute, chubby child surfaced in front of my eyes.

I immediately recalled who Tapasvi was and I was more than happy getting the news that he had cleared his NET examination. I felt proud to be associated with Tapasvi, a boy who had had sailed against the tide and managed a smooth journey.

If we go into the background of this story then, I feel I have given the same treatment to Tapasvi that I gave to any other child who came to me. I have given treatment to approximately 800 such children. Treatment can be followed easily, but the guideline that accompanies it is really difficult to follow.

When a child is born, the nine months worth of waiting results in happiness. But, if parents realise that there is something wrong with their child subsequently, then the family gets shattered.

In Tapasvi's case, his parents came to me after being dejected from many places. Now, in the case with such kids, it is really tough to determine the extent of disability in young kids. It works like a CPU and monitor; if the CPU is defective, the monitor won't work. So, CPU can stand for the brain in these kids.

Brain has three types of cells – normal cells, dead cells and physiologically dead cells (which means there are cells present, but they are inactive and they are the main culprits for most of the disabilities).

Whenever a differently-able child comes to me, I first analyse all three types of cells in them. We can't do anything about the dead cells, but we can try to revive the physiological dead cells. That too, not 100%, but between 60%-70%. Now the question arises about the outcome from that retrieval.

For that, I tried certain herbal supplements; I will not call it a medicine because medicine is something that I prescribe as a child specialist. You may call it an interest or an innovation of mine. My father was an Ayurvedic doctor and I learned certain nuances of herbs and herbal medicines from him.

Once I had met a sage who prescribed certain herbs for brain development in children and I jotted it down on paper. A couple used to come to me for the treatment of their child. I asked the couple to get certain herbs crushed and asked them to bring them back. They came back the very next day and I mixed the herbs in certain proportions, instructed them to give the mixture regularly to the child in addition to the allopathic medicines that I had prescribed. The couple came with their child after a month and when I met the child, I couldn't recognise him. There was tremendous improvement in him. I knew it wasn't because of the allopathic medicines alone, because I had been prescribing them to the child since a long time.

I believe god always paves a way forward if we are deeply interested in accomplishing something.

I got a laboratory to work in, and in coordination with Dr S.S. Agarwal, I worked on three patients. When I saw positive results in all three of them, I learned that these medicines can't be given in hyper profusion state but only in hypo state. As in, they can work towards the revival of physiologically dead cells. In these cases, the mother is the main pioneer.

Also, a positive approach matters the most. In most of the cases, the first reaction of parents is denial; they are not ready to accept that their child is disabled and I feel that doctors are in a way responsible for this denial. Imagine taking the differently-abled child to the doctor and hearing the reply "there is no solution to this problem." Such responses force the parents into not believing that their child is special.

The second cause of this denial is schools and their admission policy. The differently-abled kids do not get admission in schools easily. There are mainly three types of disabilities that come in our purview in this context – Cerebral palsy, mental retardation and Down syndrome. Mental retardation can be cured, Down syndrome can also be cured up to an extent and the toughest one to work upon is cerebral palsy. Cerebral palsy demands the maximum involvement of parents and not all parents are ready to put in that much of efforts. It all starts from the moment the child is born. In case of Tapasvi, he didn't cry when he was born; he cried very late and that might be a reason behind the state he is in today,

I have made a book of milestones and I ask all the parents who come to me to observe and mark all the points given in the book very minutely. It helps me in analysing a child's growth and development. I did the same with Tapasvi.

Tapasvi's case was different because his parents were involved fully, they didn't budge from any challenges or duties. Not all children are that lucky. Also, our country doesn't have adequate facilities and laws to protect the interest of disabled people. I believe that these kids are full of potential; give them one chance and they can do wonders.

▼

Dr Anil Kumar Jain
MD DNB MNAMS
HOD, Dr P.K. Sethi
Department of Physical Medicine & Rehabilitation

"These are the sins of the previous birth, doctor sahib, that I have to face now," said the young couple in early thirties, married for nine years, having a 6-year-old daughter with cerebral palsy.

I remember they came to me a few years back, completely lost, depressed with premature graying of hairs, carrying a heavy bunch of investigation and treatment papers along with the child who was unable to stand on her own.

With my experience, I could sense the desperateness and plight of the couple. After a while, when they had settled down a little, I asked them to narrate their problem. The mother of the child, Sunanda, started speaking, continued for 3-4 minutes, and I did not interrupt. Suddenly, Arjun, the father of the child asked her to stop and cut short the story. I overruled his objection and asked him to wait for his turn. He sat quietly, but his impatience was visible from his body language. Sunanda continued for five more minutes and ended up crying. I started feeling a little uneasy. Arjun too became uncomfortable. I asked Arjun what he wanted to say. He said a few things about the child Surbhi and finally looked at Sunanda , turned to me and asked, "Will surgery help?"

During the conversation, I was observing Surbhi, who was sitting quietly, looking upset after her mother started crying. Having heard their story, I could understand that they had already been to nearly a dozen doctors and more number of temples to conduct puja and other rituals. Before I could say something, Arjun said in very desperate voice. "You are our last hope; we have great expectation from you. Please do something."

I asked a few questions from the couple to know about their social, educational and financial status. Their disturbed emotional state got revealed during the conversation. I asked a few questions from Surbhi and could judge her average IQ level, strong desire to go to school and join outdoor activities with other kids in the neighborhood.

Such stories are usual in my day-to-day practice as PMR expert for close to thirty years.

I examined Surbhi, talked to her. I saw her in a standing position with walker support. I scanned the papers and investigation reports they had brought with them. They had been to Delhi, Mumbai, Visakhapatnam and some village of Kerala for treatment, spending unbelievably heavy amount, with almost no benefit. They had also gotten surgeries on both, Surbhi's knees and ankles, forcing her to remain bed-ridden for nearly eight months.

The last doctor they visited (Neurosurgeon) advised them one more surgery involving both feet! He also mentioned that the child may need surgery at a spinal level also.

Then they revealed the main intention of coming to me. They wanted to find out the need for surgery. If yes, when to get it done and at what age of the child. Having seen the level of confusion in their minds, I started thinking from where should I start.

I started talking about the other members in their family and came to know that the couple had separated from joint family two years after Surbhi was born. Except the two of them in their modest 2-BHK, there was no other support system. They did have a house help coming for household chores every morning and evening for a few hours.

I knew I had to start from the very beginning and asked if they knew what type of disease Surbhi was suffering from.

"Cerebral palsy," came the immediate reply. When I asked what it is, they started looking at each other.

"No one told us," Arjun said in a slightly agitated tone.

I took a piece of paper and a pen to draw a diagram to explain what happens when a child is born. Why immediately after birth, a child should cry. What happens if the cry is delayed. When I finished, they looked at each other's face, felt so foolish for not knowing all these basic things. They blindly followed advises given by relatives and friends, not having any knowledge of the disease.

I then told them the treatment options available for Surbhi and made it clear that surgery had no role to play at present.

When I said that, I saw Surbhi smiling for the first time. Arjun also looked relived. I told them I would make some braces (plastic supports for legs), will teach some exercises and instructions to be followed. Our department at Santokba Durlabhji Memorial Hospital is well known in the county for these braces, which we developed in a research project under the supervision of Dr P.K. Sethi funded by Department of Science and Technology, Govt. of India.

Sunanda and Arjun were equipped with more knowledge now, which also made them very confident. They met another patient's family in the waiting area of the clinic. Theirs was a three-year-old child with cerebral palsy, one half of the body involved, along with squint in one eye and mild involvement of speech. This was the fourth visit of the child in the last one-and-a-half year. He learned to walk with below the knee braces. He used hand splint during sleep hours to prevent contractures. He made regular visits for eye treatment and speech therapy.

Seeing all this and after talking to this child's parents, Sunanda and Arjun felt a strong sense of hope. They agreed for bracing and exercises protocol. I once again made it clear to them that it is a long, slow process and requires patience. Nothing would happen overnight, in weeks in months. We took measurements of ankle and foot orthosis (AFO) with mid thigh to mid leg anterior and posterior polypropylene shell, overlapping the AFOs.

My team of physiotherapists trained Sunanda and Arjun for stretching, strengthening, coordination and balancing exercises as well as postural instructions. They were called back after ten days for fitting the orthosis. On the day of fitting, they were properly trained for use of the orthosis.

All exercises were checked again, some more were added. Entire regime with and without braces was restructured to avoid fatigue for Surbhi as well as parents. Immediate improvement in her standing posture with walker support was noticed which further reassured Sunanda and Arjun about a positive outcome to all their efforts. A very simple frame which helped her in standing was shown to them which they got made by nearby blacksmith in few hundred rupees.

They were advised to come for follow up after a month. They reported after five weeks. They looked happy and composed. Improvement in general health of Surbhi was visible on her face. On the other hand, I could also see more patience and calmness in Sunanda and Arjun.

Surbhi looked better as the tightness of muscles had reduced. Her standing posture had improved with braces. Her diet was more regulated and she had gained a little weight. Sleep pattern had become normal. The entire regime was checked again and minor changes were made. Home tuition was arranged and Surbhi displayed more interest in her lessons and puzzle games. I reassured them and advised to come after a month.

They reported after a month with good news that Surbhi could now come to standing position from sitting on a chair with the help of a walker. She could stand for a minute without walker also, balancing herself well.

I advised Sunanda and Arjun to call Surbhi's friends home from time to time, to improve her interaction with kids of the same age group.

This regime continued for three months. Her standing time without walker support increased up to ten minutes with more erect posture. She started advancing one leg with walker support, but with considerable effort, tiring her soon. I increased duration and intensity of her exercise regime. Her overall health improved and she became more cheerful, confident, performed well academically, became more interactive with her friends, started taking interest in outside word and liked watching female gymnastic on television. Both parents were now more relaxed and happy. After a month of intense physiotherapy, the day came when she could walk few steps with walker support. Parents came happily with her, distributed sweets to the entire staff. A sense of satisfaction gripped me.

Having treated cerebral palsy patients for nearly three decades I have some important observation to share.

As everyone knows, prevention is better than cure. Prevention starts right from the time a couple plans to conceive. They should try to improve parameters of health like haemoglobin, fitness by walking, consult gynaecologist in the first trimester of pregnancy. Follow all the instruction and ultra sonography for foetal well-being. Select a hospital where all facilities conducting safe childbirth are available. Paediatrician should be available in the labour room or operation theatre where cesarean section is going on.

It has become a general tendency to look suspiciously at the doctor's decision to conduct a caesarean. Attendants do not give consent for caesarean and force the doctors to conduct normal delivery. Possibility of developing complications increases several-fold for the mother as well as newborn in such a case. Immediate cry after birth is essential as child sucks air and the process of independent respiration starts to ensure adequate oxygenation of brain and other organs.

It birth cry is delayed for some reasons, less oxygen reaches the brain and other parts. Brain is very sensitive to oxygen deficiency at this stage and starts undergoing damage. The more the delay, the less the oxygenation, and more the damage.

People think that caesarean section costs more than the normal delivery. But they should remember that the treatment of a child with cerebral palsy is several times costlier, rather time-consuming and very difficult to treat.

If birth cry is delayed, then early diagnosis of hypoxic damage to brain is essential. For this, you can consult Neonatologist, Physical Medicine & Rehabilitation (PMR) expert, Paediatric Neurologist or Orthopaedic surgeon. In case of non-availability of these, paediatrician with interest and experience in handling such cases may be very helpful.

Always keep in mind that there is no amount of weakness which can delay the normal developmental milestones beyond 2-3 weeks. Delay beyond this should be taken seriously. In such cases, early diagnosis is the key to early and maximum recovery, for which early intervention therapy has to be started. Denial in such cases is usual in parents, as they relate milestones delay with weakness. The same is reiterated by friends and family as well.

The aim of treatment in cerebral palsy patients is to make the maximum use of existing capabilities to make the child as independent as possible, helping them to gear up for the usual way of life. It also helps in making them a productive member of the society and nation, restoring their self esteem.

The first stage in the treatment is counselling, of the patient and the parents, and educating them about the disease, possible length of the treatment process and maximum possible outcome. Their over expectations should not be nurtured; ground realities should be made clear to them. Problems faced by male and female patients with the passage of time are different, so it must be explained to them clearly.

Majority patients can be rehabilitated with braces, physiotherapy, occupational therapy and child counselling. Patients with below average IQ and learning disabilities require help of special educators.

Our advice to parents is to consult specialists for any problem that arises in the patient. For instance, seizures or any other neurological complication can be best managed by paediatric neurologist. Swallowing problem and constipation require help of paediatric gastroenterologist. Gynaecological and menstrual issue in a female child would require a gynaecologist. Child with mal-development of teeth should be handled by orthodontist experienced in dealing with such cases. For squint and other ocular complications, an ophthalmologist should be consulted.

Surgery has a limited role when deformity correction is needed and should be done by an expert who is experienced in handling cerebral palsy cases with a fair idea of post-operative management for rehabilitation, in case PMR expert is not available.

Facilities of post operative bracing should be available. Good quality of brace enhances results of surgery and prevents recurrence of deformity.

The decision of doing surgery in a cerebral palsy child is very tricky. The surgeon should be able to decide when to operate. Having remained involved in surgery for nearly seven years, I feel after-surgery expectations of patients, parents and relatives are rather high. Failing to achieve desired results as per their expectation creates a mismatch and can be a nightmare for the operating surgeon.

Another method of treatment which is in vogue these days is injection of botulinium toxin. Not just a very costly option, the results last for 3-5 months before wearing out. It has to be repeated every four months. Post injection bracing is also needed. At some centres, 100% oxygen therapy is also used.

Results are uncertain and variable. The fundamental defect in cerebral palsy is the patient's inability to contract and relax the right muscles at the right time to the right extent. This creates problems with walking and working. Developing socially acceptable way of ambulation and training the child for toilet is essential before schooling is started. If the child with average I. Q. is ambulatory, trained for toilet function, has no behavioural issue, then normal schools can be pressurized to admit the child.

Other children, with more severe effects on everyday actions can try for admission in special schools where special educators use innovative ways of making the child understand easily. They use toys, charts, models and games that incorporate the messages to be conveyed to the child.

Social welfare department of the Government of India and state governments have multiple schemes to help such parents, financially and by other means, such as reducing income tax, providing free wheelchairs, crutches, tricycles, etc. Various schemes to provide scholarship to needy candidates are also there. After attaining a certain age and completing education, vocational rehabilitation is also provided.

If you explore the community, you will find many patients and their loved ones suffering silently and misguided due to lack of basic knowledge on the disease and its treatment. In a desperate situation, they want to try all options suggested by anyone, often ending in the hands of quacks working with the idea of making quick money.

Denial of their child suffering from such a disease is a universal problem. Even educated parents do not accept it easily. It often leads to delay in treatment, which is disastrous.

Role of early intervention therapy is well proven. Maximum development of brain takes place in initial few years of life. I remember a doctor couple getting angry when I diagnosed their daughter with cerebral palsy, which later turned out to be severe. Diagnosis can be made on the basis of history and clinical examination in most of the cases. CT scan, MRI is needed for diagnosis only in few cases. How can this happen to us, we did no harm anyone are the thoughts that first come! Then comes the theory of sins of past birth. Other family members nurture anger against society, doctors and paramedics.

In my observation, a cerebral palsy child in a joint family system improves better and early as compared to nuclear family. In a joint family, the child is handled by many people, automatically increasing sensory input. If child is having moderate or severe degree of mental retardation (MR), then round the clock supervision is needed to prevent self-harm by the child. Hyperactive child also requires continuous supervision. All this can be taken care of in a better way in a joint family system.

School admission of CP child is another problem faced almost by all parents. Routine schools say a strict no in majority cases. Special schools are few and not well-equipped in terms of manpower and other resources. Careful counselling of policy makers is needed to counter this problem.

Physical exploitation of differently-abled population is on the rise even before they attain sexual maturity. If the child is female, the risk is several folds.

The attitude of society has to be changed and it requires change in the existing mindset. This is possible when all the concerned parties are educated about the disease and its outcome. This again requires round the clock supervision.

▼

Dr R.K.Gupta
MBBS, MD (PAED., MED.), FIAP
Fellow of Indian Academy at Pediatrics
Professor of Pediatric Medicine
SMS Medical College
Jaipur

"Doctor, when is my baby going to look at me and give me a smile?"

I looked at Prachi and knew that the day had come when I would have to disclose the grim truth to the mother holding the six-month-old baby boy. The signs had clearly been there in the past few visits.

Nothing could soften the blow to the young parents, so I said in plain words, "Your baby has cerebral palsy."

They stared at me blankly and I told them that their child was going to have some mental and physical deficit and his overall development was going to be delayed.

Disbelief, fear, agitation were evident on their faces, "Why? What happened? Are you sure, doctor?"

I tried to answer all their queries gently and made them understand the problems and difficulties they were going to face in rearing this child.

In subsequent visits, I was happy to see that Prachi had overcome her apprehensions and had whole-heartedly accepted her baby and his condition. There was now a single-minded dedication in her, to improve her child's quality of life.

After numerous physiotherapy sessions and visits to occupational therapist and speech therapist, Saksham, at the age of four years, took his first independent step. I still remember the happy tear-filled face of my patients' mother when she informed me about the same.

The mother's complete devotion to her child was evident in her child's progressive development. At the age of seven years, Saksham was admitted in a school which catered to children with special needs. Interaction with other children brought happiness and excitement in Saksham's life.

Prachi had decided that she would devote her entire life to her son. She knew having a second child would be an added responsibility and she would have to share her time, love and life between the two and she was not ready to do so.

Saksham's health had its ups and downs. He would have seizures, kidney problems and various illnesses every now and then. But with his parents' continuous care, he became healthier and more independent in his day to day activities.

Being a doctor, I have seen many such patients, and looking at them, I can say that every such child is unique and special in his or her own way. Our joint efforts can bring fulfillment in the lives of these children so that they can find their special and deserved place in the society.

In my experience, whenever I have told any parent that their child is suffering from cerebral palsy, their first reaction is that of denial; they are just not ready to accept the condition of their child. "Doctor, you must be mistaken", this is the dialogue that I have heard in all the cases where I have diagnosed and treated these differently-abled children. I don't blame the parents for this reaction, the society is at fault. The acceptance starts from the parents and moves of to both the maternal and paternal family, thereby reaching out to the society. If there is a hindrance at any of these levels of acceptance, that becomes the starting point of the problem. We as a society should accept that the mother is in no way responsible for a differently-abled child, especially not in case of cerebral palsy. The parents are already tensed and anxious after the diagnosis, and at that time, blame game doesn't come out as a very healthy option.

These special children can do wonders, they just need a healthy environment and a chance to prove themselves. Give them a chance and opportunity to fly high and they can prove to be surprisingly wonderful.

Dr Swati Sharma MDS (Periodontics and Implantology)
Professor, Dept of Periodontics
Mahatma Gandhi Dental College, Sitapura, Jaipur

Children represent the future of our society and ensuring their healthy growth and development ought to be a primary concern for all. Someone has rightly written: 'judging a child who has special needs doesn't define who they are....it defines who you are'.

As a dentist and a periodontist, I frequently encounter and provide dental treatment to children with special health care needs. A child with special needs will always inspire you to be a special person and managing such patients makes you realize your strength, tenacity and resourcefulness. Every child matters and every child has the right to a good start in life. So is the case with children with special needs.

The dental management of such children creates doubt and anxiety among dentists. This theme is highly underexplored throughout the undergraduate course and we do not have enough theoretical foundation to work on this field. This can be achieved by additional training as well as increased awareness and attention, adaptation and accommodative measures beyond what are considered routine. Children with special health care needs include those with behavioral issues, developmental disorders, cognitive disorders, congenital or genetic disorders or systemic diseases. These disorders place them at an increased risk of various dental problems and thus it is very important to establish preventive health strategies at a very early stage. Understanding the child's oral condition and implementation of preventive health strategies helps in effectively managing the oral health of the child. It is generally seen that such children have poor oral hygiene and increased prevalence of cavities in their teeth, along with various gum problems. This leads to compromised eating habits, leading to nutritional deficiencies. The parents, burdened with medical treatment and costs, do not seek dental treatment. Moreover, the importance of dental health has often been overlooked by health planners.

The dental condition of children with special healthcare needs may be directly or indirectly related to their disabilities. Growth abnormalities and medical conditions adversely affects their oral health. In addition to this, these oral diseases may also have a direct and devastating effect on the general health of these children. As I previously mentioned, such children are highly prone to dental decay. There are various contributing factors for this. Uncoordinated chewing may leave a lot of food in the mouth and inadequate cleaning by the tongue due to improper muscular control may further aggravate this condition. Also, such children reside at home and are pampered with a variety of sweets and junk food, by their parents or caregivers.

In addition to this, they suffer from xerostomia (decreased salivation) leading to inadequate cleansing and are generally advised high sugar content syrups, which make them more susceptible to decay. The second most frequently encountered problems faced by these children are gum diseases. They generally complain of bleeding gums, bad breath, loose teeth and ulcers in the mouth. There is difficulty in performing proper toothbrushing due to reduced manual dexterity leading to the above-mentioned plethora of problems. In addition to these commonly encountered problems, they also suffer from white spot lesions, delayed tooth eruption, mal-aligned teeth, various anomalies in size, shape and colour of teeth and various habits like night grinding.

Management of such children starts right from the time the child enters the clinic. It is generally carried out in 3 phases. The first phase aims at relief of pain and control of further spread of infection, following which the treatment is carried out for the underlying disease in the second phase. Finally, planning is carried out to prevent further disease from progression in the tertiary phase.

The oral examination of children with special needs is similar to those of normal children. However, one might encounter increased gagging, *uncontrolled muscle movements and motor incoordination during the treatment. The treatment plan for such children is also the same as others, but may be done with more patience and making them calmer by giving some medicines. Daily home preventive care may be tailored according the individual child's needs. They include fluoridated toothpastes and fluoride or antimicrobial rinses in addition to use of motorized powered brushes. Fluoride application should be considered as a preventive tool in such cases. This can be done either professionally at a dental clinic or at home. Dental sealants are a good preventive option for such children to prevent the onset of dental problems.*

Here I would like to share one such experience with a child whom we patiently handled at our clinic. The child named Hrithvik (name changed) reported to our clinic with a complaint of bleeding gums, bad breath, mobile teeth and difficulty in chewing food. The parents had consulted a nearby dentist for the problem, but the treatment was of little help. Since I am a a Periodontist (to be more precise, I specialize in treatment of various gum problems), this case was referred to me for better management. The moment the patient walked into my clinic with his parents, I could sense that there is some problem with the gait and behaviour of the child. The child exhibited difficulty in walking, uncoordinated muscle movements and had overactive reflexes.

When the child started speaking, there was some stuttering in his voice. I made the diagnosis of cerebral palsy, which was later confirmed by the child's parents and his medical reports. The oral examination was much time consuming since I needed to identify the areas according to their disease severity. As I explained the diagnosis and treatment plan to the child and his parents, which included multiple visits to the clinic, they were initially reluctant. They agreed after I explained in detail about it. Then started my battle of delivering a proper treatment and managing the child at the same time. One noteworthy thing which requires special mention about this child was that he was highly motivated for the treatment and exerted maximum cooperation from his side. This further motivated me during the entire treatment and kept my spirits high. I took 6-7 sittings for cleaning his teeth in contrast to 1-2 sittings which we usually take. I had planned for a flap surgery in the second phase of treatment but was not able to execute because of involuntary muscle movements. We then shifted to plan B, which included deep scaling, curettage and root planing under local anesthesia. Administering LA was a huge challenge for me during the entire procedure since there is high risk of injury to any part in the oral cavity. The gums bled and bled during the entire treatment, but it gave me immense satisfaction as I saw the gums turning from bright fiery red to reddish pink and then finally health pink gums. The child and the parents started confiding in me and became more sincere in following all the home care instructions. It gave me immense satisfaction on seeing him effectively using the powered tooth brush and following all the oral hygiene instructions. I feel more contented when I see him smiling with confidence.

To conclude, I would say that general health and oral health go hand in hand. Children with special needs are more prone to oral diseases which can adversely affect their quality of life. Dental care for these children has been given less attention by parents and health professionals. Let us all join hands and be aware of our responsibilities and services for these children as they certainly deserve the best that medical and dentistry has to offer as an important part to their total habitation. A child with special needs will inspire you to be a special kind of person. Sir Stephen Hawking has rightly said, "And however difficult life may seem, there is always something you can do. In the end, it matters that you don't just give up."

▼

Dr Manish Gupta
MBBS, MD (PMR)
ESIC Model Hospital
HOD, RRC

A few months ago, I met an old friend of mine who is now married and has a fourteen-year-old daughter. Her daughter is suffering from cerebral palsy. As we sat down for tea, she said it is a result of her past karma, or maybe the sins of her previous birth that she is facing and living in every moment of her life.

During college days, she used to be a very jovial, enthusiastic girl, but now she was all transformed, more concerned about her daughter than herself. She told me that her daughter was premature and was born by operation. At the time of birth, the doctors told her that her child was going to be different, but she didn't understand it then. As my friend and her husband were gifted with their first child, a daughter born prematurely, they didn't take the doctor's saying seriously and went for Oxygen Therapy in NICU for a long time, near about a month from her birth. After a few months, she came to know that her child is actually different as the doctors had predicted and was suffering from cerebral palsy. She told me that her mother-in-law loved her too much before this child was born, but after her, her mother-in-law left her all alone to take care of the child. One the other hand, she loved her daughter a lot and dedicated her whole life to her. She wanted to make sure her daughter enjoyed life just like other children.

As a couple they tried everything they could do for their child. They went for long term physiotherapy sessions continuously for ten years, which were truly helpful for their daughter in many ways. She learned to walk, sit and speak certain words through them. They also went for oxygen therapy sessions which are not pocket-friendly for a middle class family, went for opinions of various doctors across the globe only to find out that it is a non-curable condition in which only the degree of severity can be lowered.

With regular physiotherapy, their daughter started going to a school for differently-abled kids named Disha. After that, she could use the washroom by herself, eat her food from the plate, understood some words and developed a love for colours.

"My daughter has an artistic side to her. When god takes away one ability of yours, he bestows you with another one. She paints really beautifully. I intend to exhibit her paintings one day to motivate others," she told me.

Another incident which is close to my heart took place when I was doing my residentship from SMS Medical College Jaipur. A patient named Rohit, son of Mr Surender Singh, came on a wheelchair. He must have been around five years of age and complained of tightness in legs. He was unable to stand and walk, couldn't even sit without support or maintain body balance. But nothing could kill the smile on his face. He was quite chirpy and had a charming persona. Although he couldn't frame complete sentences, he *used to ask me repeatedly in broken words, "Uncle mein kabhi chal paunga kya" and I used to reassure him every time of a positive outcome.*

According to his father, they didn't know till the initial one year after the child was born that he was suffering from cerebral palsy. They thought him to be a normal child, but even after one year, when he didn't show his milestone behaviour, they took him to the family physician. The physician conducted certain tests, after which his condition was confirmed as cerebral palsy. Their physician explained each and every condition that Rohit might have to face in the near future. But Rohit's parents were not ready to take it and started visiting various temples and hakims in hope of a miracle. They also tried other medical practices, but found no noticeable results. After losing hopes from various sides, Mr Surendra came to us with his five-year-old bubbly kid. We did a few investigations and after that the kid underwent thigh and leg surgery. After a time span of around one month post-surgery, the kid was able to stand with support of walker and calliper. The physiotherapy sessions continued for about a year for both the upper and lower limb as his upper limbs were also tight and stiff.

Many a time after that, he came to the hospital with his father to meet me and I found a significant change in his physique. Now he is able to walk a few steps on his own. His physiotherapy sessions are continuing till date but there is a remarkable change in the child.

I shared these two real life incidents so that others get hope out of it. It your child is born different, you or your child's life doesn't stop there. There are roads to travel to and mountains to climb. You just need to have the determination and the positive outlook to face the adversities. A differently-abled child can also do wonders, provided he gets the required support and infrastructure to achieve his dreams. These kids have very good IQ, what is needed is the background support to nourish it.

Love them, care for them and treat them as one of your own , and you will see their smiles making their life journeys easier.

4

Tapasvi's Schooling Challenges

Tapasvi was already experiencing schooling at home, even before we enrolled him in a real one.

His school started at 5:30 a.m. sharp. I would wake him up, keep a place mat near his bed so that when he kept his feet on the floor, he didn't catch a cold. I would make him wear his slippers and take him to the washroom.

While brushing, I would start the day by clinking his water jug with a brush to mark the countdown. From 6:00 a.m. to 8:00 a.m. was the exercise time. Simple exercises that would help him improve strength in the arms, to improve his grip and move his legs. I used to make him hold pencils, asked him to differentiate between the types of beans and assigned him other small tasks to enhance his day to day movement.

The initial school to which Tapasvi and Manasvi were sent was Roserary play school. I didn't sleep even a minute on the night before Tapasvi was supposed to join his seminary. I knew that the time had come when Tapasvi would realise that he was different from others.

I didn't know how to mould my child so that he could face the brutal world, that was going to judge him for almost everything. Since both my wife and I were working, my parents used to take care of Tapasvi for the entire day.

The play school to which my kids went was a happy-go-lucky place, with lots of swings and toys to play around with. More than Manasvi, it was Tapasvi who was thrilled to join the school. It was the first time Tapasvi had seen the world outdoors. It was my mother who used to take the kids to school. Manasvi used to be in her arms while Tapasvi accompanied her in a pram. In the school, while Manasvi could move around anywhere, Tapasvi was confined to a chair.

Getting calls from the school became an everyday affair because the staff didn't know how to administer such a child. One day, my mother requested if she could leave the pram in the school. The school administration bluntly refused.

That night, my mother cried a lot, thinking about how dependent Tapasvi would be on others forever. To her worries, my father always responded, "Believe in god! I am sure almighty will protect him from all the challenges."

We understood the true meaning of our father's words as we progressed forward in the journey of Tapasvi's life. It has taken the help of a whole lot of people to mould Tapasvi into what he is today, as Tapasvi beautifully puts it, "I am a beautiful painting painted by various artists."

▼

I wanted Tapasvi to not just attend the school, but to learn. For that, the support of the whole family was required. For society to accept him, acceptance of family was the foremost to be achieved. Once Tapasvi got exposure to society, his learning could begin.

I never let my kids think that there was anything they couldn't achieve. I have always inculcated the vision of 'you walk ahead, I am right behind you' in them.

Once, there was a fancy dress competition in their school. I wanted Tapasvi to take part, but had my own set of dilemmas about how Tapasvi will minister his stage presence. Asking Tapasvi not to take part was not a possible solution, and I didn't want an excuse as a route for my child. Finally, I decided to make Tapasvi a balloon seller and stood behind him on the stage, holding an assemblage of balloons in the same attire and get-up as Tapasvi.

Tapasvi came on to the scene on a wheelchair. I walked right behind him till the centre of the stage. The whole school was assembled there – the students, teachers and even the parents. And here I was, a man of thirty-five years, standing behind his son on the stage in a fancy dress competition, holding balloons. I didn't have any inhibitions in doing so; it made me feel complacent. It was the first time Tapasvi went on stage, faced a crowd and made his presence felt. That was clearly another step forward for the father-son duo.

Once when Tapasvi came home from school, he didn't seem to be well. On further enquiry, he told us how he had broken a thermometer in his mouth in the school. He had a fever in school and the medical staff put the thermometer in his mouth instead of his armpit which was customarily done in case of kids. The school staff didn't even bother to inform us.

My wife called me up and briefed me about the whole matter and without wasting any time, I started off towards home in a jiffy. On the advice of Dr Sunil, he was admitted to the hospital and kept under observation for twenty-four hours.

Mercury is a dense hot liquid, capable enough to melt your insides. Tapasvi was already feeble. What if something happened to him in those twenty-four hours?

Although by god's grace, nothing happened to Tapasvi, that incident was an eye-opener for us. We realized that we had to be very scrupulous with Tapasvi.

Manasvi continued in the same school, but we took Tapasvi to another school. It was always the same problem everywhere, Tapasvi needed support with basic functions like turning the page, opening his bag, opening his lunch box and nibbling. And no school had these facilities which was essential for a differently-abled child.

During those days, special schools were not even heard of, at least not in Jaipur. Uprooting our lives and relocating to some metro city was out of question since we had our respective jobs with Government of Rajasthan.

While other kids in Tapasvi's class could go out in the playground during lunch break or during prayer hours, Tapasvi used to sit alone in the class. One day, I caught a glimpse of Tapasvi sitting alone in the class, with him staring at the kids outside in the playground. It broke my heart.

As my kids were growing up, it was becoming wearisome for my mother to take care of the kids. We employed a young girl to take care of my children. But, one day my mother saw that the girl was eating my kids' food sitting on our bed while my kids were left on the floor in the chilling month of January. We asked the girl to leave at that very moment, realizing that our kids couldn't be left with anyone except family members.

But one person who turned out to be different from the rest was Ms Parul, who used to come for teaching basic concepts to Tapasvi. I am not exaggerating when I say that she played the role of a second mother in Tapasvi's life.

She started off with teaching Tapasvi the basics such as how to draw a line and a circle. Tapasvi's first letter and word could be credited to Parul ma'am's hardwork. She just didn't play the role of a teacher in Tapasvi's life. Rather, she took care of him like a family member.

We had tears of happiness in our eyes when one day we saw her cleaning Tapasvi's drooling with her own dupatta. It was an indication that the world outside was ready to accept Tapasvi the way he was, without any judgment.

Parul played the role of a mentor, an elder sister in Tapasvi's life. Manju found an accomplice in Parul, one in front of whom she could ventilate all Tapasvi's imperfections without the fear of being judged. The patience that Parul displayed while handling Tapasvi was commendable.

But the moment we thought that the worst was over, we were in for another problem. Try to visualise a situation where a guy with cerebral palsy holds a pencil for the first time, trying to write letters in the books and the letters seem to be flying away from the pages.

Primarily, we thought it to be a fantasy Tapasvi had created in his mind, but when he kept saying the same thing over and over, we decided to take him to the doctor.

"Mr Sharma, I am really sorry but your son suffers not just from cerebral palsy, but from dyslexia too." These words of the doctor echoed in my mind for days, giving me no clear perspective of what lay ahead. I was seeing an obstruction at the end of every turn that I was taking and that's when Parul ma'am governed the situation.

"Ajay sir, I cannot guarantee you of the end results, but I will endeavour with my full capacity." With these words, and an unparalleled dedication and conviction, she started teaching Tapasvi. Parul ma'am wasn't trained or equipped to handle special children like Tapasvi. She wasn't aware of any exclusive teaching aids that she could use with Tapasvi, but we saw warmth and affection in her eyes. She had a zeal to conquer her challenges, and she embraced our problems as her own too. Although the progress was painfully slow, we saw a gradual momentum in Tapasvi's advancement over a period of a few months. A dot turned into a straight line, thereby forming a circle after three months.

I still remember the day Tapasvi wrote his first letter "A", I was elated. We knew we had won the initial battle, but there was still a war that lay ahead.

Straight from the heart

As special educators played a crucial role in the development of Tapasvi as a person, here is a first-hand account from someone special.

Parul Jain
Lecturer, Commerce
Tapasvi's First Teacher

My journey with Tapasvi dates back to around seventeen or eighteen years from today, when I visited Tapasvi's home for the first time. I still remember that scene vividly, a cute chubby child clad in white kurta pyjama with sparkling eyes was sitting with his arms open wide, trying to come into my lap.

That was Tapasvi's way of welcoming me into the house and the family. I don't know why, but when I saw Tapasvi for the first time, I felt as if I had known him since ages. It was around those days only when Tapasvi had started going to school. He was in LKG then and I started with teaching him the Eglish alphabet, Hindi letters and numbers.

In the initial days, I was quite nervous because I wasn't sure of myself. I did not know whether I would be able to teach him or not, but with the passage of time, slowly and gradually, Tapasvi made that task easy for me. He started learning himself.

Tapasvi's grasping power was and still is very strong. He has been a sincere student, someone from whom I never got a no for any task assigned to him. Along with Tapasvi, his whole family used to get involved with him in his everyday activities, especially his father whose day used to start with Tapasvi's exercises and end with a walk supporting Tapasvi.

Tapasvi had a working mother, still she never left any of her duties unfulfilled or undone. His twin brother and Tapasvi used to fight a lot. Tapasvi used to shout at an extreme pitch when he was in a state of anger, but I have seen that anger melting away in seconds. Tapasvi has been really lucky in terms of family support, whether it is from his parents or grandparents or his brother.

One thing I have observed is his father's attentiveness towards Tapasvi was that he always used to listen to Tapasvi's point of view in every matter, however trivial it may be.

Tapasvi's father got a special table constructed for him that would fit with his physical structure. I used to reach his home at around 5 p.m. and I always found him ready for his lessons at his table. I had to derive innovative strategies to teach Tapasvi so that he could learn quickly.

For example, in the chapter of addition and subtractions, we started off with counting and writing numbers on his fingers thereby adding his fingers. If I had to make him learn something in languages, I used to carve a story on the spot.

One remarkable thing about Tapasvi is that I never had to teach him any topic twice. He was so sincere and dedicated that his full concentration used to be in the subject while studying. It has been a two-way relationship with Tapasvi; we both have taught each other and I have learnt a lot from him. His everlasting smile despite his physical limitations, his spirit of playing till the last ball and his confidence are some of the attributes which make him stand apart from others. We had a deep understanding between us. So much so that whenever he used to learn something new, I used to be really happy, as if I had learned a new topic that day.

Going to teach him was like therapy for me and I didn't want to miss teaching him even for a single day. I really used to look forward to teach him something new every day. Initially, our progress was a bit slow. Even after one month of our class, we were stuck at 'A' for apple and the number 1.

But with time, we picked up and there was no looking back. Actually it was the will power, zeal and spirit to prove himself which motivated Tapasvi to study and learn new things. Gradually from 'A' for apple we moved to reading and writing sentences and then paragraphs.

Tapasvi's family treated me as one of their own. I still remember the festival days when I used to celebrate with them. Today Tapasvi has reached a remarkable position in his life and I feel really proud of him. That small chubby boy sitting with his arms outstretched has done wonders with his hard work and dedication. I feel blessed that I was able to play a small role in his journey. He proved himself despite all the setbacks; he considered his problems to be the stepping stones of his life. I wish him all the love and blessings to rise higher in his life.

5

Tapasvi's Learning in School

Mr Sharma,
This is to inform you that we will not be able to admit your child Tapasvi Sharma to our school.

Other parents get rejection letters when the child enters into a college. In Tapasvi's case, the rejections started rolling from the first standard itself.

I appealed to every school in Jaipur city to enrol my child, but all of them rejected the application without even having a conversation with him. I was tenacious about giving him a proper, formal education, but where could I possibly send him?

There was no school which was ready to admit him. All the big schools claimed to admit differently-abled children, but reality was very different. I tried getting Tapasvi into many of these schools, but no one admitted him, saying that they lacked the staff and resources to support him.

Sometimes, the school would take him for seven days but they would send him back home with a reparation letter, stating:

Sorry Mr Sharma, your ward cannot pursue his education in our school.

There was no explanation given from these schools. It was just these piles of letters that followed. These letters stripped me of my confidence, but more than me, they broke my child. Here was a small boy who had battled cerebral palsy and dyslexia to be able to read and write, and even after all his efforts, he was being turned down.

In the face of all these rejections, I thought Tapasvi was getting dejected too. It was a natural conclusion, as I was in the same frame of mind.

But in due time, he proved me wrong. In lieu of giving up or breaking down with us, he got galvanized to prove himself. For once I thought about giving up on his education and trying to focus on the physiotherapy. There was a nagging feeling in my mind that when he'll be able to walk to the school, none of these institutions would rebuff him. Would not say no to admitting him to the school. But Tapasvi did not agree with my assessment of the situation. He was hell bent on getting a proper education.

During one of the bi-monthly visits to the physiotherapist, we got to know about an NGO and a school for differently-abled children. Without wasting any more time, we went to visit the school. It was perfect for my child. It had slopes with handlebars on the top to enable children to walk on their own. There was a physiotherapist available, along with a competent medical staff. But there was another issue; there were no openings.

The school had reached its maximum admission capacity and there was no scope of any new admissions. I pleaded, but in vain. Eventually, they offered me a home course on how to teach your child at home.

We used to be called to the school monthly and were coached on how to take care of a child with cerebral palsy, dyslexia and other disorders. While his education started shaping up by then, we never lost our focus on his physiotherapy. Tapasvi was taken to a speech therapist to help him with his ineptitude to swallow and to control his drooling, Parul ma'am meticulously worked upon his writing and we concentrated upon small gimmicks of his daily life.

I wanted my child to be complete, I wanted him to know everything and I wanted him to have friends he could talk to.

▼

After a time span of about six months, we got a written communication from the school stating that Tapasvi could now officially join the school. The epistle stated that we had to buy books and a new school dress for Tapasvi. It is rather strange but the small event of buying a new school dress brought great happiness to me.

Tapasvi was really happy the first day he returned from the school. The school was a positive, vibrant place full of lush greenery. It had lots of swings and toys that were specially designed for differently-abled kids. It had paintings on the walls and specially contrived seating arrangements.

As Tapasvi started his new journey, time became a major concern for me. Since everything with Tapasvi took double the time and effort, I started losing out on certain tasks that I had to complete. I wanted to pay attention to Tapasvi's growth, wanted to give my whole time to him, but that was not something I could do at leisure.

There was physiotherapy, Tapasvi's school, my office, my wife, my parents, my family and another child to take care of. I had started feeling that everything was taking a backseat because I was too busy concentrating on Tapasvi. Till date, I give the whole credit of taking care of Manasvi to my wife. I cannot imagine how Manasvi dealt with this experience as a child, of getting most attention from one parent and only some from the other. He must have felt left out, untended, but he never once expressed it. Perhaps that is how we all sacrificed a bit of ourselves to make up for what Tapasvi was not given by nature.

With the passage of time, I started becoming more occupied. I didn't have any time for myself or for Manasvi. Tapasvi had always been an assiduous child, but could not accomplish tasks without assistance. As time started becoming a major constraint, I started feeding Tapasvi as we walked about in the house, holding bars. I would read the newspaper while doing exercises. When I left from office, I called up my wife to get a glass of water and a cup of tea ready for me, so that I don't waste any time. Given the value of time as we had come to see it, even a phone call seemed like a waste of time.

Inevitably, I found myself getting cut off from my social circle, simply because I could not afford to devote time to them. There was nothing in my capacity that I did not try with Tapasvi. I would mix kidney beans and garbanzo beans for Tapasvi to sort to work on his eye-hand coordination, a pot would be kept medially in his legs to make sure they do not intersect. I ligatured a pillow to his legs at night so that the day's exercise did not go waste.

At an age when the other kids were unearthing new toys to play around with, my child was handling exercise instruments. I made him do some sovereign activities, took him for horse riding, swimming classes and even made him walk in the sand which was quite impractical for a guy suffering from cerebral palsy. Now when I look back, sometimes I feel that I overdid a few things. He never complained, never uttered a word, but I shudders to recollect what all he underwent because of the insistence with which I compelled him to succeed. I felt I was becoming everything my son needed – a father, a mentor, a guide, a therapist, a doctor, a trainer, a tutor. In all this rush, I forgot to become his friend.

Although Tapasvi's mind works undoubtedly well, he couldn't read as he suffered from dyslexia and squint eyes. In those days, there was no internet, no reading aids available which could spell out the book for him.

Manju and I became Tapasvi's reading aids as we took turns to read books out to him.

Tapasvi was not able to turn pages because of his physical limitations. To solve the issue, I went to a school which was built for visually impaired children and was located in Kishanpole, Jaipur.

There, I met a young boy who introduced me to a particular software that could scan the book and then, the books could be read on the computer. With the help of scanned images, Tapasvi's problem was settled, but only up to an extent, because Tapasvi was suffering from dyslexia too.

When god takes away something from you, I believe he makes up for it by giving something special in its wake. I feel god made up for Tapasvi's lack of physical strength through his sharp mind. Tapasvi has a really strong memory; his recollection and remembrance capacity is as hard as nails. We didn't ever have to read out anything to him for the second time, and he never crammed up anything. He understood the basics, shot counter questions and made sure he understood things thoroughly. Which is how he fared so well in his exams. At that point of time, it used to mar our throats after speaking so much, but it was nothing in comparison to what a child suffering from cerebral palsy and dyslexia was doing – he was keeping all the ammo intact in his brain.

Once Tapasvi was enrolled in the school in the first standard, he started commuting through the school van. Kids with all sorts of special needs used to accompany him.

I sometimes found Tapasvi acting like a source of motivation for other kids in the school to do better.

We have encountered all sort of people in our journey. When Tapasvi used to step down from the school van, there were bystanders who used to stare and there were neighbours who used to lend a helping hand, but none of them wanted to know more about his predicament.

I fathom that people in general are not aware of conditions such as cerebral palsy and dyslexia. I have always tried to share whatever knowledge and experience I have gathered on this with whoever who wishes to know more. All that I ask in return is for them to have an open mind while meeting my child. I have seen people be judgmental, and I have also seen Tapasvi work hard for the simplest things that we usually take for granted. So I just ask people to not spurn my son by just one look at him. Do not surmise that he won't amount to anything because people with such conditions do not.

With the passage of time, I realized that physiotherapy was important, but at the end of the day, his education would help him go farther in life. All this time, he had been an astute child, scoring above 85% in all examinations.

Although the school was good, things did not go as well as I had anticipated. While the staff was trained enough for taking care of differently-abled children, the educational quality was not what I had expected.

"What more do you want, Mr Sharma?" the principal asked me, and I didn't have an answer.

I wanted more. I wanted him to touch the moon and the stars. But right now, I was again seeing a blocked road at the end of the turn. A change of school when Tapasvi had already settled in was a grave challenge, but we knew we had to take this one.

It was also during this testing time that Tapasvi turned into an atheist. I remember when we went to a resort for a trip, there was a small temple within the premises of the resort. When Tapasvi tried to enter the temple, the guard asked him to take his crutches off.

Tapasvi reiterated that he could not take his crutches off otherwise he would not be able to walk, but the guard didn't budge. Since that day, Tapasvi hasn't put his foot inside any temple.

Dyslexia

Not many are aware that with Cerebral Palsy come other challenges, sometimes hidden behind the veil of cognitive disorders. Let's read more about them for a better understanding of Tapasvi's challenges.

As per the common understanding, Dyslexia is often identified as a reading disorder. Also affecting individuals with normal intelligence, it is characterized by difficulty in reading. Its effects differ in degree from person to person and cover a broad spectrum of complications like – problems in spelling words, reading, writing similar-looking words and letters, differentiating between spellings of similar-sounding words, and drawing a quick connection between words as one hears them, reads them and writes them. It takes time to spot dyslexia-related symptoms, typically until school starts.

Alexia is a condition in which an individual loses their ability to read, and this is not a birth defect. Such individuals possess a natural desire to learn, but cannot after a while, because of difficulty with involuntary movements. Dyslexia, on the other hand, is often caused by an interrelation between genetic and environmental factors. It is associated with ADHD (Attention Deficit Hyperactivity Disorder). There is a high rate of ADHD in dyslexic children. While some cases of dyslexia are genetic, others develop because of other reasons like stroke, or dementia, identified as acquired dyslexia. An individual diagnosed with dyslexia primarily undergoes issues in the brain's language processing area. Hearing, visual problems, and other deprived teaching opportunities that trigger reading disabilities are not the same as dyslexia. Diagnosing dyslexia after careful observation require the conduction of a series of tests that study the individual's memory, vision, spelling and reading skills.

One of the foremost treatment methods for dyslexia comprises an adjustment in their teaching methods that matches their level of understanding. However, this isn't a cure for the disorder, but only an attempt to minimize the symptoms. Symptoms that interfere with a dyslexic individual's vision aren't credible.

According to the latest records, almost 3-7% of the world's population suffers from dyslexia, making it one of the most prevailing learning disabilities. In fact, around 20% of other individuals not diagnosed with this disorder may also exhibit some negligible symptoms. Dyslexia affects both genders equally, but more number of men have been diagnosed with it so far. A group of scientists and medical professionals prefer calling dyslexia another existent learning style with its pros and cons than just labelling it a disorder.

Classification

There are two distinct classifications of dyslexia – developmental and acquired. Developmental dyslexia is the type that develops during a child's early years. Dyslexia caused by neurological abuse or an injury or trauma to the brain is called acquired dyslexia. Some signs of acquired dyslexia and developmental dyslexia are similar, but the methods to evaluate their extent and treatment are different.

Signs and symptoms

Diagnosing dyslexia late, even in childhood, could lead to some typical symptoms of low phonologic cognizance and retarded speech development. People often misunderstand dyslexia as the disorder in which individuals write backward or mirror the writing. These are not defining signs of dyslexia as several dyslexic individuals overcome these reading and writing issues using appropriate learning methodologies.

A lack of phonological awareness gives rise to reading and learning disabilities like identifying or generating rhyming words or counting the number of syllables in words. Children with dyslexia might face difficulty in understanding specific sounds of a word or blending sounds.Another complexity of this learning disorder includes poor spelling memory identified as dysorthographia or dysgraphia, a condition depending on orthographic coding. Such children also find it challenging to retrieve the names of things. Symptoms of Dyslexia, which also include the inability to read at grade level spill into later ages of adolescence and adulthood.At that stage, the person cannot comfortably recall, memorize, read aloud, summarize, or learn foreign languages. Even though adults with dyslexia possess decent communication skills, their reading speed is slower, and they don't perform well in spelling tests and reading different words owing to less awareness of phonics.

Associated conditions

It is typical for Dyslexia to associate with other learning disorders, but there is not much information about this comorbidity. A few associated disabilities of dyslexia include:

- Dysgraphia: A poor hand-eye coordination could cause complications in writing or typing. This condition is called Dysgraphia, which also interferes with the individual's ability to identify the direction, conveniently partake in sequence-oriented processes like repeating tasks or tying a knot. Weakened letter-writing automaticity, organizational and elaborative difficulties, and decreased visual word forming are factors causing dysgraphia in dyslexia. Children, therefore, find it challenging to recover pictures that spell a word.
- Attention Deficit Hyperactivity Disorder (ADHD): ADHD and dyslexia are some of the most found association disorders. Individuals with ADHD act impulsively, are hyperactive, and also cannot sustain attention. Figures show that 12-24% of people who have dyslexia also have ADHD, and almost up to 35% of people diagnosed with ADHD also have dyslexia.
- Auditory processing disorder: Auditory processing disorder also co-occurs with dyslexia, impacting the processing of auditory information. It could also interfere with the child's auditory memory or sequencing. The problem is common

in many children with dyslexia, who later become capable of creating logographic cues that help them overcome this impairment. Research also claims that these skills are the main deficit in dyslexia.

- Developmental coordination disorder: Developmental coordination disorder associates itself with dyslexia, which is a neurological condition. A child with dyslexia and developmental coordination disorder has characteristics like difficulty balancing, controlling fine motor skills and using speech sounds. They also undergo the issue of short-term memory.

Assessment tests

Assessing the presence of dyslexia necessitates a collection of tests in educational and clinical settings. On finding signs of dyslexia in the first round of tests, doctors then conduct another round of diagnostic tests to identify the extent of dyslexia, its type and other associating disorders. There are different methods to conduct these tests – on a computer by a teacher, or specialized training as recommended by psychologists. Some of these tests are also equipped to offer teaching methods to help the child overcome learning difficulties. These comprehensive tests determine all cognitive, behavioral, emotional and environmental factors that contribute to the child's learning impairment. The results of these tests could offer different observations:

Tests like the Wechsler Intelligence Scale for Children, Woodcock-Johnson Tests of Cognitive Abilities, or Stanford-Binet Intelligence Scales offer a general estimation of the child's cognitive abilities. If the test identifies low general cognitive ability, the child would face more difficulty in reading. These cognitive ability tests also test the individual's verbal ability, non-verbal ability and spatial reasoning, working memory, and processing speed. Only psychologists perform these tests, which also differ for different age groups. One requires special training to give and score in them.

As per prominent researchers, there is still no proven identification of the pattern of these cognitive tests that confirm or eliminate different reading disorders.

- Screening or evaluation for mental health conditions: Caretakers involved in the lives of dyslexic children can fill out or complete checklists that characterize the child's emotional and behavioral patterns. Older children comfortable with reading can themselves take the assessment because the checklist for parents, teachers and young children is the same. Screening or evaluating mental health conditions can be carried out using the Behavioral Assessment System for Children and the Strengths and Difficulties Questionnaire. To further evaluate and research these symptoms and compare them with children of that age and gender, these forms include nationally representative norms.
- Screening checklists such as the Vanderbilt ADHD Rating Scale, the Screen for Child Anxiety Related Emotional Disorders (SCARED), etc., provide insight into specific psychiatric diagnoses. While these tools assist with the identification of possible disorders, they also run the risk of producing false positive scores (i.e., indicating the presence of the disorder even when the individual does not

really have it). Hence, these checklists must be supported with standardized psychometric tests and/or diagnostic interviews. The prevalence of anxiety and depressive disorder is two-three times more than conditions like dyslexia. Similarly, ADHD is more common than other conditions.

- As for dyslexia, the average spelling /reading ability scores of percentage rank below 16. Hence, when reviewing academic achievement and skills, psychometric tests in addition to the grades and teachers' notes are recommended. Standardized psychometric tests can be administered at a group and individual level.

  For example, a teacher can conduct the Iowa Tests of Educational Development in a group/classroom. However, tests like the Wide Range Achievement Test or the Woodcock-Johnson Test (including achievement tests) are administered to individual students by teachers who have specialized training in overseeing them with manual-based instructions.

Screening

Children who show signs of dyslexia undergo screening tests to confirm the disorder. Although, no test works better than an examination of the parents' and biological sibling's medical history conducted in the child's preschool years. Screening tests conducted involve primary school teachers observing pupils (between the ages 5-7) showing signs of dyslexia, especially their grasping power of phonics and learning speed. Screening tests like the Phonics screening check, currently used by schools in the United Kingdom, follow next.

Child and adolescent psychiatrist M. S. Thambirajah emphasizes, "Given the high prevalence of developmental disorders in school-aged children, all children seen in clinics should be systematically screened for developmental disorders, irrespective of the presenting problem/s," when observing medically. This renowned psychiatrist Thambirajah recommends these screening tests be conducted when children show developmental disorders, including dyslexia, and after examining the child's developmental history. Having a school report of the child's academic and social performance and a psychosocial development examination are also suggested.

Management

It is a myth that individuals with dyslexia can never read or write. Compensation strategies, therapies and educational support offer the required support to dyslexic people, so they can independently read or write. Some proven techniques and technical aids also extend help with managing and hiding the visible symptoms of dyslexia. One such method is to keep the individual away from stress and anxiety, which has a positive impact on writing comprehension.

Interventions for dyslexia include the use of alphabet-writing systems. Such interventions attempt to help the child connect the letters (graphemes) with their sounds (phonemes). Once the child connects them, they are shown how sounds blend into words. Finally, the child applies this connection in reading texts and spelling the words. Such a parallel practice of application in reading and spelling simultaneously offers longer-lasting benefits than mere training in understanding phonics. Furthermore, such an intervention provided early on helps reduce reading failures.

There is no scientific or medical proof that special fonts like dyslexie and open dyslexic ease reading difficulties. But there is proof that dyslexic children can comfortably read regular fonts like Times New Roman and Arial as comfortably as children not diagnosed with this disorder, after taking up some learning techniques. Many such children have preferred these regular fonts over the specially-tailored ones. However, increasing the space between letters using regular fonts is an advantageous reading technique.

Society and culture

Society even today doesn't fathom and accept any disorders due to a lack of complete information. But it was worse in the 1980s when people considered education the cause for dyslexia than understanding it as a neurological disability. Even today, a large group of people look at children/people with mental disorders differently, and misjudging their condition, not just socially but also at workplaces. The stigma could disturb people undergoing these disorders, who may lack a positive atmosphere and warmth. Children and adults with dyslexia should compulsorily have instructors who also help them cope with living in such an environment where they are looked at differently, so that it doesn't further impact their learning progress.

Reflections from the Educators

With each step that Tapasvi took in the world of education, there was something new to explore. Let's hear it from someone who stood by him each step of the way.

Epan Chako
Umang School,
Jaipur

When I met the students of class nine of Umang in the year 2011, I had no idea that among the rough stones some gems are waiting to be polished and exposed to the world to shine. I was asked to try taking classes in social science for the students. The class had a strength of ten. My efforts to teach them resulted in the realization of the fact that seven out of the ten students were not comfortable with the task of learning the voluminous syllabus. These seven students opted out and took up painting instead. This development allowed me to sit with this small group of three in a corner of the class and give personal attention to each. This was yet another chance to assess the strengths and weaknesses of each of my students.

It did not take much time to understand their aspirations in life. Tapasvi had a clear vision to study well, get degrees and become an IAS officer. He was always confident in interacting with visitors and expressing his opinion on topics of public interest – be it politics, sports or anything of social significance. His insistence on studying social science for the tenth and history for the twelfth board examinations, respectively, and history and English for his graduation overcoming the pressure to take up law for his graduation shows his clear vision for the future and his determination. I greatly admire this trait in him. Even though he was getting special attention and admiration in the school and from the public, he never sought to take advantage of the opportunity. I doubt that he chose to live without any special status at home also, notwithstanding the occasional fights for his rightful place in the realm. He is still keeping up his efforts for the fulfilment of his dreams.

Reports of domestic discrimination – where the so-called abled child is unduly given all sorts of facilities, whereas the special child's birthday is ignored and not to speak of any birthday gifts – are shocking. Every demand of the abled child is fulfilled without any hesitation, whereas the genuine demands of the special child are ignored. I presume our case study is an exception. It is untiring efforts of a few among the special people who could gather enough courage and resources and those concerned with the welfare of this neglected category that finally got them a percentage of representation for admission in educational institutions as well as in employment.

Even though there exists no reservation in representation to various legislative bodies from the Panchayat level to the parliament, there are some eminent persons belonging to special categories in parliament as well. We have a lot of public figures who work to improve the conditions of special persons in our society. It is because of their untiring efforts that the Persons with Disabilities (Equal Opportunities, Protection of Rights and Full Participation Act, 1995) was passed by the Indian Parliament, recognizing the existence of special people in the society and the need to protect their interests by providing for their adequate representation in education and employment. It also provides for the creation of a barrier-free environment, rehabilitation and unemployment allowance for the differently-abled.

This could be seen only as small step in the right direction when compared to the fact that in some Western countries, the government has taken up the full responsibility of children with special needs. Let us also look forward to such a situation in our country, when the full responsibility of bringing up special children is taken up by the government, so that no special child in our country is deprived of an opportunity to discover and nurture his/her abilities and make full use of it.

I am sure Tapasvi will make full use of his talents and opportunities to achieve this goal for the welfare of all the special people in our country.

6

Tapasvi's Social Influences

I always wanted to make Tapasvi aware about who he was as I firmly believed that self-awareness was the key to growth and development.

I consciously enlightened him about the nitty-gritty of his medical condition. I did not want him to be dependent on anyone to make his decisions. That is why I never imposed my choices on him. We ensured to involve him in family matters so that he develops independent thinking capability. As parents, we wanted to give him a free environment where he could explore and express his individuality.

Once Tapasvi recognized that his voice was being heard, he felt more confident and self-assured. I wanted to give him limitless exposure. I did not want to confine him within the four walls of the house. I wanted him to go out and enjoy nature in its pristine form – feel the wind in his hair, taste the snow and feel the dew drops on the grass.

On some level, I knew I was aspiring for something which seemed unattainable – how could my child, a patient of cerebral palsy, experience all these moments when he couldn't even walk properly?

But, I had never learnt to give up, however dull the situations. As a family, resilience was truly in our DNA.

I used to pick up both the children in my arms and take them to museums, forts, parks and entertainment zones in Jaipur. It may sound bizarre, but I even took Tapasvi to a discotheque once, just to make him experience what it looked like. I used to take him to dog shows to make him learn about the various dog breeds. I took him to Jaipur Literature Festival so that he could absorb diverse ideas and enjoy fascinating stories.

Although it was a tedious task, I took him to buy grocery so that he could observe day-to-day phenomena. It used to be a difficult to get Tapasvi down from the car, make him clamber up the steps to the grocer's shop and create a place for him in between the crowd at the shop. All this while, we used to attract strange looks from the onlookers, but that did not deter me or Tapasvi for living our life unapologetically.

I took him to the escalators in the malls, just to let him get a feel. Sometimes, I even took him for auto-rickshaw rides and let him choose his clothes while shopping.

Tapasvi used to be at the back of my mind even during my office hours. I started feeling as if we are one soul living in two different bodies. If Tapasvi was hungry, I used to feel hungry. If Tapasvi was drowsy, I used to feel like sleeping. If tapasvi was depressed, I felt gloomy. If tapasvi was jubilant, I felt more exultant than him.

▼

The one thing that was different, though, was our religious faith. I used to firmly believe in deities. Having faith in god gave me the strength to fight all odds. And then, with time, I did not realise when my faith turned to superstition. I started seeking assistance from *babas* and *gurus*. One such instance left an indelible impact in my life.

In those days, there used to a man called Mr Shiv who was believed to have cured specially-abled children in one day. One of our close family friends suggested us to go and meet him as he knew certain people who were positively affected by his treatment. I tried contacting Mr Shiv, but he wasn't giving us an appointment.

We decided to visit his office in Jaipur. Built on a vast expanse of land, he had his photographs depicting him in various sessions that he had conducted in different cities.

One of his followers told me that he was going to conduct a session in Udaipur after seven days. This time, without taking an appointment. I decided to go and meet him. The session was being held on the outskirts of Udaipur. We reached there sharp at 7:00 a.m. but even after arriving early, we saw that the place was overcrowded. Our turn came at around 2 p.m. We were escorted into a room which was lustrously lit. It looked very grand and impressive.

When Mr Shiv saw Tapasvi walking with the help of crutches, he asked me to remove them.

"But sir, without these crutches my child will not be able to walk," I said.

Mr Shiv assured me that it was the last time that my son would be walking on crutches. He would not need them again in future. When I heard those words, I was overwhelmed with joy. My emotions overpowered my reason as I touched his feet. He then asked me to leave the room.

What happened next was unbelievable! He came near Tapasvi and shouted loudly in his ear. After that, I was called to take Tapasvi out of the room. That was his way of curing my child. Tapasvi was still on crutches when we came out. There was media surrounding us. They asked me if my child was cured and I replied in affirmation. I was scared that if I don't say yes, then his treatment might not work.

We came back and waited for his treatment to work, but it didn't. Tapasvi was using crutches. My story was published in one of the articles about Mr Shiv next week. I was mortified to read my statement. I decided to never take that path again. Tapasvi was a major force who bought me out of that vicious circle.

▼

Tapasvi had a problem in sitting properly or sitting cross legged. It was strenuous for him to uphold his balance and therefore, he used to sit in a W posture which was strictly opposed by the doctors. It was because regular posture of a cerebral palsy affected child in W position weans off the effect of physiotherapy.

One evening, when Tapasvi was about five years of age, I came back from the office, only to find both the boys sitting in a W position. I was so furious that I pushed him onto the floor.

"What you think you are doing", I shouted. I was so angry that no one tried to stop me. I have spent every moment of my life, trying to make Tapasvi's life better and yet, when I was not around, he was being careless.

I felt quite unsettled and shaken up. But that was the critical moment when my child concluded that there was something seriously wrong with him.

That day, I made them sit next to me and told him about his medical condition.

Imagine cerebral palsy being explained to a five-year-old, but I had to do it. I told him everything – the challenges he would have to face, the activities he would not be able to perform and the different life he would have to lead. I did not want to demotivate him. Rather, I wanted him to know the truth so that he could prepare well for what lay ahead of him.

Tapasvi could not afford to spend his time loitering around with the toys. He had far greater things to accomplish. He was too fond of cricket, but he knew he couldn't play on the ground.

He was so passionate that he had learnt every intricate detail of the game.

It was one of those moments when life gives you a choice--either go forward and make the most of what you have or wallow in self-pity and give up. Tapasvi was not easy to be defeated. When he found out he won't be able to play cricket, he figured a way out to be in the game. He chose to be an umpire for the cricket games that happened around him.

▼

There are two kinds of people in this world – Those that see you drowning and deflect. And those who see you drowning and offer help. Tapasvi had to learn how to judge people in order to decide which set of people were good for him.

To counter that and make sure he became aware of people, we had to take him out so he could meet more people. We decided to take Tapasvi to various social events. It used to expose him to all kinds of people. We have dealt with situations where small kids used to touch Tapasvi and run away as they were afraid. Sometimes, he used to be treated as if he was some object you could play with. But with every interaction, Tapasvi evolved!

Reflections from the Educators

Bhavana Sharma
Special educator (MR)
Chandigarh

Nowadays we are evolving so quickly that we have no time for others. No doubt modernization is at its peak, but we are accepting it without giving it a thought. We are doing things because the other person in front of us is doing so. But then I see the same people – who are so eager to learn about other's culture – not even focussed on their children, I cannot understand. Yes, I'm talking about children with special needs.

While I was in school, I saw this special school for children. I used to think how this could make any difference. Sometimes when I used to take that particular road for my home, I was just scared, I didn't know why. But after post-graduating, I decided to do something very different.

Something that may help the society. I was there at the counselling for my Bachelor's in Education, when I chose this particular field and studied it for two years.

Children with special needs are no different than the other children, so why is there this gap? They are just differently-abled. I came across the fact that some of their families have just left their children to be in hostels. Just because they cannot accept the fact that they have a special child, they send the child away from them to hostels so that they can live without them. In all this, they forget how important family is, for these children. I don't know whether they go and meet them in their hostels, but what I'm sure of is that they are missing one of the best experiences. The main reason that I think they leave their kids in hostels is because acceptance of these special children in their families is hard and difficult to admit. They just don't want to believe that the child they have is a special one. They are in denial that this could happen and usually taunt the mother for such anomalies in the child. They forget that it has nothing to do with her. The lives of the special children become much easier if their parents are co-operative.

In India, people are less aware about special needs, therefore they don't know what to do with the special child. People are more in favour of superstition that some baba's tantra-mantra can help their child. They have to understand that nothing can change them. It's their normal and parents have to accept that. Instead of going in denial, they should search for the therapies that can help them and their child to cope up with the situations they are facing.

If the special child is a boy, they will somehow try to manage, but when it comes to a girl, the family can be super ignorant and blame the little one for every single mistake that she does. When the girl reaches her adolescent age, she has to suffer more, not only because of the behaviour she's in but also the changes which start occurring in her body. It is much more difficult for her to manage. It's not easy to make them understand that the changes occurring in their body will eventually be a routine.

People in western countries are not only more aware of these disabilities, but also accept them. They help their child with all possible therapies that are beneficial. In these countries, they are equipped with all the things they need because they know how to handle such patients and their parents.

When I decided to join this special course, I just wanted to have a professional degree, but working with them made me realize that it doesn't matter what professional degree you have, what courses you've opted for. What matter is the fact that I always ended up putting a smile on their faces, which I think is more than anything that I could have done.

While I was teaching during my course of special education, I came across many reasons for a child to be differently-abled. They are absolutely adorable children because they are different. Working with them and teaching them was difficult because this field was new for me. But eventually, it all went along and I was happy. It was worth it. Choosing this field and working with them made me realise that no matter how grown-up you are, you will always be a kid at heart. I consider it a great privilege that I had the chance to interact with such amazing children. Society has labelled these kids as incompetent, less human, and even dumb, but I am here to tell you that special kids are quite the opposite. They are unique in their ways.

A child with autism, cerebral palsy and dyslexia is like any other special kid. A kid who needs attention like any other child.

These children are anti-social and repetitive in their behaviour because of autism, but that's okay. If you can understand them and help them, nothing will stop them. Their viewpoint of seeing things is different. It's not difficult to understand what they want to say. Once you have made up a good reputation with them, they are always yours. While teaching, I understood the fact that once they open up to you, they will always surprise you in their different ways. In ways you cannot imagine.

One must do something for someone in order to bring a smile on their face. That someone can be anyone in your family or in your locality or just a differently-abled child. Treat everyone with kindness.

7

Tapasvi's Excellence Soaring High

It is aptly said that almighty opens the second door if he chooses to close the first one. This is exactly what happened in case of Tapasvi's education.

One of the teachers from Tapasvi's erstwhile school, Ms Deepak Kalra decided to start his own academic centre for differently-abled kids, an educational institute which the city of Jaipur really needed. The school started on the ground floor, in the house of Ms Bina Kak, former Tourism Minister of the Government of Rajasthan, with kids sitting on the floor and studying.

And that's when the parents took charge and provided resources to make the school more effective. Some bought the desks and tables from their house, others bought toys, books and all other stuff that they could manage. A group of parents, teachers and students collectively named the school Umang.

Umang had a very crucial role to play in changing Tapasvi's life. If there is one educational institute that I give credit to for Tapasvi's refinement, it would undoubtedly be Umang. Starting from the fifth standard itself, Tapasvi studied in Umang for eight years thereafter, passing out in twelfth standard. Umang gave him the much needed confidence to let go of his hesitations and reach his maximum potential.

Umang gave Tapasvi a chance to merge with others who were like him. After interacting with these kids, Tapasvi came to terms with his own reality. With Umang, Tapasvi competed in debates, extempore, skits, speeches, science olympiads and a lot more.

Once there was a painting event in which one of Tapasvi's juniors had to exhibit a painting. On the day of the competition, the kid befuddled and then, Tapasvi was called by the teacher to present that painting. The judge was so impressed by Tapasvi's dog and pony show of the painting that she declared them the winner.

During Janmashtami, Tapasvi delivered a speech as instructed by the school authorities.

Dr Shailendra Singh, who was the guest of honour that day, was so fascinated by Tapasvi's performance that he invited Tapasvi to his house to interact with him personally.

Another time, there was an inter-school skit competition in which Umang was enacting the acclaimed play written by Rabindranath Tagore called “Kabuliwala”. Tapasvi wasn’t a part of the skit, but he used to help his friends during the practice sessions.

Two days before the skit was supposed to be staged, Tapasvi was offered the role of the protagonist, Kabuliwala. Within two days, Tapasvi committed to memory the lines of the play for which the other kids were practising since the past one month. He sat in front of the mirror till he perfected his expressions. The moment he entered the stage, I couldn’t even recognize him for once.

Tapasvi even attended Shiamak Davar’s dance classes in 2006 for two years. Once while attending a conference on child abuse, Tapasvi was asked to speak in the end as an extempore. I was accompanying him to that colloquium. I was anxiously feeling that Tapasvi might not be able to give an on-the-spot speech, but he proved me wrong. He spoke for ten minutes straight, without any pause, without any notes.

He quoted data and statistics and that was the day when he stopped using any notes for his stage presentations. All these accomplishments are not something unusual for any other child perhaps, but for a kid braving cerebral palsy and dyslexia, these small things mean the world.

At another instance, Tapasvi also participated in an inter-school competition where a team of three had to talk about consumer awareness. All three in Tapasvi’s team played their part really well. After the evening, a question-answer interaction round was promulgated at the request of the audience. Even the teachers were sceptical about such an instantaneous announcement, but Tapasvi took charge of the sphere and answered each question with such a flow that he was called over as a guest speaker next year.

In the words of the teacher accompanying the trio to the event, Mrs Bakshi, "Tapasvi's conceptualization was so clear that he didn't falter for even an instant. He was calm, composed and dauntless at the same time, a rare personality trait to see in kids of his age."

But that day, Tapasvi was hurt when people told him, "You were superb, we didn't expect it from you". People not expecting him to be brainy, astute or capable pinched him the most. Cerebral palsy or dyslexia are not benchmarks of judging the capability of any child, but people are quick to judge, aren't they?

Umang is affiliated to NIOS, National Institute of Open Schooling that caters to needs of a heterogeneous group of learners up to twelfth grade. In 1986, the National Policy on Education proposed strengthening of open school system for extending open learning facilities in a phased manner at secondary level, all over the country, as an autonomous system with its own curriculum and examination leading to certification.

In Umang, every class has a small group of students so that equal attention can be given to each student. The subjects and syllabus is tailored as per the capability level and special needs of the students. Some of the students like Tapasvi, who cannot write or do not have pace of writing because of certain physical hindrances, need a writer too. During the early years, Tapasvi used to write in exams, but as the syllabus became complex, Tapasvi's writing speed didn't match with the subject matter and he started taking the help of a writer.

Here, I would like to make it clear that the writer is not given by the school, nor is there any app or website where the writers can be scoured for in cases like Tapasvi. A writer has to be in a lower class than Tapasvi and be able to write quickly. The writer should also be able to comprehend what Tapasvi is trying to dictate while writing the examination.

When it came to searching for writers, it has been a roller coaster ride. Sometimes I got three writers at once, at other times not a single writer was available. In case of some important exams, I had to keep one writer as a backup

In the words of Tapasvi's school principal, "Tapasvi has been quite a focussed guy, beating all odds with his indomitable spirit and doggedness. He has always wanted to be ahead of his present station, ahead of his time, in fact. He has accepted and beaten every demur, have aspired for the stars and reached there."

Tapasvi had been quite a prominent figure among his peers and classmates, owing to his 'never give up' attitude. In many situations, I had seen Tapasvi boosting the morale of his classmates when he himself was feeling down.

Let me tell you something – not every differently-abled child is accepted by the society easily. The reason for it is simple enough; parents themselves are not too keen to accept their child. Some of them just lock up their children in their room, make sure the child is clothed and well-fed, and feel that their duty is over. They feel humiliated in introducing their specially-abled family member to the world. I could never understand what thought goes behind such a behaviour. After all, the child is your creation, you brought the child into this world. So how is the child accountable for the state that he is in?

Tapasvi has met many such children through multiple NGOs and I have seen him emerging and standing in support of such children. He has, in fact, urged me to do something for these kids many a time. I am proud of my child for the fact that he can forget his own challenges and extend help to others.

Umang had always encouraged the students to go out and interact with the society. As a part of the educational module, Tapasvi addressed an audience of more than a hundred people once.

I was sceptical about Tapasvi facing such a large crowd, but Tapasvi broached his speech with full elan,grit and clarity over the subject. There were people who had apprehensions over his proficiency and intelligence, but Tapasvi's chutzpah made all their doubts melt away. All those who cross-questioned him or asked him to chronicle a particular topic for the second time, he answered with full command over the subject and proved them all counterfactual.

Tapasvi has an aura about him. If you meet and interact with him for once, you can't take him out of your mind.

His classmates often grumble that he takes away all the heedfulness of all the girls in his class, thereby diminishing chances of others. After Tapasvi completed his matriculation, I wanted to mushroom his exposure. I wanted him to go and study in a normal school, but again, I was met with repudiation. Differently-abled children aren't able to camp on the doorsteps of higher studies generally, lack of disable friendly colleges being the main reason for it. There were a lot of times when Tapasvi wanted to learn a particular itemized subject, but no particular teacher was on deck, especially in case of history, a subject which Tapasvi dotingly refers to as his first girlfriend.

At that time, one of the parents, whose child was a friend of Tapasvi in Umang proffered to teach Tapasvi and moulded the way for Tapasvi's future. He is till date one of the most revered teachers of Tapasvi, Mr Epan Chaku. Tapasvi was the only child he taught. He made some really practicable notes for Tapasvi, which were useful for him even in his post-graduation. Other than history, Mr Chaku worked towards improvisation of English language of Tapasvi.

Once my friends came over for dinner. I have a close-knit circle of seven friends of mine and we customarily meet once a year. Whichever part of the world we maybe in, we come to India as a part of our get together. That day, Tapasvi talked fluently in English with all of them, leaving them in awe of him. I was thrilled to see my child brimming with mettle in a dialect which is not even his native language. These little jolly moments innervate me to put another foot forward with Tapasvi every new day.

Reflections from the Educators

Deepak Kalra
Director
Umang School, Jaipur

When a child comes to Umang, the first step is assessment. You know, identifying all the areas in which there is special need, the areas that require an opportunity to develop. Six people are involved in this process and we start off with the neurologist. After we get a report from the neurologist after the medical diagnosis, our own physiotherapist, occupational therapist, speech therapist, special educators test the child individually. Now that's our ground on which we start an individual education plan for each child. If we find that the child has good IQ scores and he will be able to cope with academics, we plan a programme in which they go into academics. They may need some physical exercise or support from school, just some support or grip for handwriting so we combine all that and we put together all the specials needs with the curriculum that the individual child has to follow. That is how the original education plan is formed.

The children are grouped into small groups, basically trying to make them as homogenous as possible, so that we can also work one to one. There are a lot of advantages of being in a group, so we try to make groups according to the ability of a child and the kind of programmes that they are going to get. I think age doesn't matter much, though we try not to combine very varying ages. There are some people who have repeatedly asked me if we make these groups according to IQ, but that's a big No. There are a lot of other things like the social and emotional aspects also and based on that, we form groups.

There is an assessment at the end of every year and the child is not compared to other children, but to herself or himself. As in to gauge, what a particular student was in the beginning of the year and what he/she has achieved. It is ok if you have not achieved all our goals; you can repeat some of them for the next year. For example, if the child has not been able to understand some chapters of seventh standard, we would carry them forward to eighth syllabus. There are lots of mediums of learning, so we don't just leave it to the classroom. A lot of other methods are also used, whether it is drama, sports, music, dance, outings, whatever we feel is going to help in learning. We don't restrict just because they have special needs or maybe some of them can't walk properly or talk without the teacher's help… that doesn't stop us from helping them climb the mountain. It is like breaking that barrier that one would have in terms of a person being differently-abled. People impose so many restrictions just because they see a child isn't speaking as well as they are speaking. They don't realise that this child is developing much more than them in many other ways and I have seen a lot of people get surprised when they are beaten down by these children in various activities.

If we talk in terms of parents or social structure, acceptance is a very, very difficult thing and it's not that if you accept somebody once, it is forever. Tapasvi was a very different story because of the kind of family background and the parental support he got. Acceptance is not easy; it takes a long time. When the child is very young, all parents pass through a lot of phases – the first being denial. They don't want to believe that the child has disability.

Then, when they find out the medical condition, the emphasis is on blaming and how the child got this physical abnormality in the first place? Who is responsible for it?

Then they start looking for a cure, they want the child should undergo some operation or medication to make the child absolutely fine. It takes a lot of time for parents to understand that it is not a disease. It is a condition and there is no cure. There is only management. You will not be able to undo the damage that has been done, but whatever residual ability we have, we can work with that and go a long way. So once that comes, that is our first step of acceptance, then the parents start working towards providing opportunities to their special children.

Again, acceptance keeps changing, it is very easy to accept a small, little child who is very cute in your lap. You can play with the child or a toddler. Then the child starts growing and becomes physically big and you still have to do a lot of management with them. You see the child in their adolescence, growing up and getting hormonal changes, you have to reaccept the child and then again you have to reaccept the child once they are in college and they get attracted to the opposite sex which is a very natural process.

Every stage of the child's life requires acceptance all the time. So if you have accepted this small, little toddler in your lap, it doesn't mean that you have accepted this child forever in your life. A lot of parents find it easier to accept young children but as the child grows older, the parents also grow older. When they were young, they were more confident of handling their child, they were physically more sound. As they grow older, the child's needs they become bigger and the parents become weaker. That's when they have to reaccept the child. Without a doubt, it is tougher with a girl child who is differently-abled; it is almost like a crisis when they come to puberty. It is like chaos and panic, the parents become worried for many things. The management of few days when the girl is going through her period is rather tough. So right from something as simple as how to physically manage it to what consequences that it can have to fears related to it, also development of secondary sexual organs plus the safety of the girl is daunting for the parents as well as the girl. So they become worried on many issues, especially for those who are severely challenged and have lot of physical problems, physical issues and are not independent – like a lot of autistic girls do not like the feel of a pad; they just take it out and throw it. You just cannot use logic with them because they are very sensitive to touch and they do not like the feel at all. With a normal child, the method that you use is explaining what it is and you understand the process why this is happening to me, but if there is a child who cannot understand why it is happening to them, they try to get rid of it and don't cooperate with parents in the management. All of this can be managed, though the parents will have to take out some extra time for their children.

A lot of parents whose girl child is severely challenged do want to go for hysterectomy which in our country is illegal. It becomes a very big issue for the parents and they cannot go for the surgery and are not able to manage this condition.

In India there are so many cases where not just the in-laws, but even the man finds it difficult to accept the specially-abled child as his own. There are ego issues and they think it isn't possible that they have produced a differently-abled child. They would always say that in our family we do not have anybody with such condition. Unfortunately, if the delivery took place at the maternal grandparents' house of the child, then hundred percent, total blame is put on the mother of such a child. Even if the delivery takes place at the man's house and everything is handled by that family, they will try and find out ways of finally putting the blame on the new mother. This kind of attitude is rather common. A lot of people think that well educated, intellectual, upper status kind of people may not be like this, but what I have seen is that education, your financial status and your urban status has nothing to do with accepting this situation.

This acceptance is very individual and there was a case of a family of a differently-abled child in a rural area. They loved their child so much, that the whole family including the neighbours used to get involved in providing the physiotherapy so that the child can walk. There is such wonderful acceptance of the child from those people. Some of them have never been to school, but accept the child whole-heartedly and give whatever help they can.

On the other hand, you see a set of parents who are highly qualified, placed in some of the top companies or maybe government jobs; there are people who are doctors or IAS officers. They have education, financial status and everything that can give them an enviable position, but they are not ready to accept the child.

The most important factor in working with such a child is how much of yourself you are ready to give. The amount of input that you need to give is much more than a normal parent because you have to address a lot of special needs apart from all the needs of a regular child. It can include the need for education or socialisation, the need for outings or for food, etc. Apart from these, you have a set of special needs that require a lot of input and for a very long time.

If we talk about acceptance, I find parents accepting the child's condition, but are not ready to give. They just want to send off the child to school and they feel they have done their part and everything should be taken care of in the school. At home they give excuses like the child does not work with us, does not listen to us, I have this problem or that and I do not get time. They just find excuses and they do not want to give more to the child. That has a major impact on the child's development and growth. Tapasvi's case was exceptional – if he used to brush, his father brushed with him, even if it meant brushing twice for his father. If Tapasvi used to eat, his father used to eat with him, even if it meant eating double. So he had eventually found his ways and I don't expect all parents to be able to give that much.

Tapasvi's parents are one extreme end, and majority people fall in the moderate category. There are still a lot of them who just don't do anything to help. In school, we can only work with the child once a day and as a parent you have to work with the child two to three times at home. I have tried to explain to parents that the child is almost there. You have to just give therapy and within six months or within a year, the child will be able to start walking on their own, but then also the parents don't work with the therapist.

Walking is a game-changer for not just the specially-abled child, but the family as well. Because if you have to carry the child and do everything physically for the child, it is very different from the scenario when the child is physically independent. I have seen people not working for such a major milestone as well.

In some cases, I have seen that the parents get so carried away by the input into this child that they neglect the second child. That, again, is wrong because you have to have a balance. It is quite common to see this happen, and the other sibling gives you a lot of indicators but parents mostly just ignore them. They start acting like their differently-abled sibling to get attention from their parents.

Sometimes parents give more attention to the other child and ignore the special child completely. Getting a balance is extremely important and it takes time because the sibling also grows and passes through a lot of phases of accepting their reality. They also have friends who do not have a differently-abled sibling; so right from accepting that I have a sibling who is different to not wanting their friends to come home, to not wanting the sibling to come to their school to not wanting anybody to see their sibling and not wanting anybody to know that they have a sibling who is special – these count as the stages which the sibling undergoes.

It starts with something as basic as comparing and they also take time to accept why this happened, why I have a sibling like this, why can't my sibling be like the others. Like parents go through the 'why me' stage, so does the sibling. They are reported to have more sibling rivalry all the time. It takes a long time to adjust with the reality and hand, and finally when then grow up, they turn around full circle. With age comes understanding and they can accommodate their special siblings better in their scheme of things. Some of them have very healthy relationships, especially girls. They get into nurturance very quickly, which boys don't. They encourage their sibling to be their playmates, play games with them, go for outings, working together, watching television, entertainment and just doing things together.

There are lots of studies done on post-parental care. It is really interesting to see that even in a country like ours – which is basically a patriarchal society, with the male member inheriting everything – girls came forward and take charge of their special sibling after the parents. The same has not been seen with boys with respect to their specially-abled sisters. Though this is not always the case.

Sometimes the first born turns out to be differently-abled and we encourage the parents to go for another child. In this whole process of planning another child, the parents are rather worried.

In my tryst with such families, I have seen about thirteen twins in Umang where one is healthy, and the other has special needs – just like Tapasvi and Manasvi. There are seven cases of siblings in Umang where both the brother and sister are differently-abled. In fact, I have one case where there are three. In such cases, I find that the parents become numb to the situation and they just shut a particular part of them which hurts too much.

They have to cope with the situation at hand and end up working like machines and as teachers we have to be very careful when we deal with them. At times they ignore a lot of things and they don't do a lot of things. I have seen two ways in which families react – either they come too close and they get together to bring up the child. Or, some couples drift apart. Because of the lack of acceptance, there is a lot of bickering and blaming. Also, a single parent handling the child is very common too. This happens when the other parents drifts off somewhere else, doesn't take responsibility.

I have also seen broken homes where one of the parents has left, not always the father. There was a student's mother who just walked out of home saying that she can't take this responsibility anymore.

We have had two cases where the parents committed suicide. A lot of parents go through phases of anxiety in their lives all the time and you can see all those phases coming; you can see depression coming, but they work it out and they get over it.

In India, it is a very unfortunate thing that going for counselling for depression is a taboo. More than a taboo, people don't realise the importance of it. If they have a physical illness, they rush to the doctor but in case of psychological issues, they do not recognise it. Even when it is pointed to them, they do not want any help; they feel they are capable of handling it on their own. It is in cases that become extreme that we see an increased level of stress and anxiety. It is imperative for parents to accept their child's situation and stay mentally strong.

8

My Glass Child

One of the books which had a profound impact on me was *Sita's Sister* by Kavita Kane.

It revolves around Urmila, Sita's sister and the untended wife of Lakshman. I believe that she does not receive the kind of attention that she deserves. Her inner strength, endurance and sacrifice are extraordinary.

As Sita went into exile, her younger sister stayed back at the doomed palace of Ayodhya. She could have accompanied her husband, but she did not. She agreed to be left in the palace, even though it meant for her to be separated from her beloved husband.

Everyone talks about the forfeits of Ram, Lakshman and Sita but no one commends Urmila for her unconditional love and sacrifice. Even after living away from her husband for fourteen long years, even after taking care of the whole clan for fourteen long years in the absence of her husband and sister, Urmila isn't worshipped.

Neither do we find temples of Urmila, nor is she revered like other mainstream gods.

But, why am I telling you this? Because, every time I think about this book, it reminds me of my own child, Manasvi, my 'glass child'.

Glass children are siblings of a person with disability. They grow up in a home with a sibling who takes up a disproportionate amount of parental energy. The word 'glass' is used because people tend to see right through them and focus only on the person with the disability.

During one of our appointments with the physiotherapist, we met a Russian couple. We got along with them really well. In fact, in the midst of one of our coffee sessions, they said, "While it is great that you are leaving no stone unturned for Tapasvi's upbringing, ensure that Manasvi isn't left behind."

Those words struck me as I felt that it may be too late. I had already neglected my younger child. Manasvi was closer to Manju while Tapasvi connected with me more. Over time, I realized where I was at fault.

I vividly remember when the kids were around eight years of age, Tapasvi was an ardent cricket fan while Manasvi had already started representing the school football team. One night, both of them wanted to see their favourite sport on television.

A day before the scheduled matches, I overheard them bumping heads over the remote as they were arguing which sport will be played on the television. I knew that owing to his physical attributes, Manasvi would win and Tapasvi might lose out on an activity which he truly enjoyed. Therefore, I unsubscribed the football channel when they went to school the next day.

I still remember the disappointment that Manasvi faced when he could not find his football channel. Ultimately, he gave the remote to Tapasvi and went to his room, without saying anything.

Sometimes you have to make hard choices as a parent. I knew, as a child, Manasvi was conscious that he didn't get the attention that he deserved from his father and it was tough for him to digest this fact. He even became slightly rebellious in his teenage and started diverting towards his friends. I was upset to see how his mother had to tolerate his tantrums, but I couldn't do much.

Today, when I look back, I realize that it was neither Tapasvi, not Manasvi who was at fault. We were trapped in unforgiving circumstances. I didn't realise back then, but now, I accept that there had been certain predicaments that Manasvi handled in a very graceful manner.

When guests used to come over, they asked for Tapasvi. Every award that Tapasvi received, I used to show it to the visitors with pride. Manasvi had been a marvellous football player; he had represented his school and university in football. When he was selected to play for the state, he was supposed to go to Dehradun, but it wasn't possible for me to accompany him.

I just couldn't afford to leave Tapasvi and go because I knew his mother will not be able to execute on her own.

And so, Manasvi couldn't show up at the training; he was not a part of the team anymore. That day I saw anger and dejection in his eyes. I would have been elated to see him on the field making his way with the ball towards the goalpost, but it couldn't happen. I had failed him.

Now, when I look back, I feel that in the course of devoting time to Tapasvi, I became a little prejudiced towards him. Both my kids had been achievers, but I never highlighted the achievements of my younger son.

Manasvi was a very brilliant football player. Had I paid a little more attention, he might have represented the states or the national team, but I was too preoccupied!

In graduation, Manasvi opted for law. We had a heated discussion on his career choice as I wanted him to study physiotherapy for the sake of my elder child.

Today, I realise that I was being so selfish. I did not care about Manasvi's passions, inclinations and ambitions. Rather, I wanted him to become an extension of Tapasvi, his shadow. I was stripping Manasvi of his identity while supporting my other child.

When Manasvi didn't agree for physiotherapy, I forced Tapasvi to join law college. To my dismay, Manasvi became a pillar of strength for Tapasvi. Maybe, staying together for nine months in their mother's womb had something to do with it.

▼

Tapasvi had lived most of his life confined to the four walls of our house or the school. All his teachers, relatives and even friends had met him in our presence mostly, because he needed an escort. We talked at length with Tapasvi's teachers before appointing them for Tapasvi as he couldn't be left alone with anyone. There was an English teacher, a young lady who used to teach him in the afternoon, when both Manju and I used to be in our respective offices. Manasvi used to take care of Tapasvi during those hours.

On the third day itself, the teacher asked Tapasvi to lend her some money, saying that she was in dire need of it. Manasvi overheard the conversation, but he didn't react as he was waiting to see how Tapasvi would respond to the situation. Tapasvi gave her the money. Manasvi followed the lady to know if her problem was genuine, but she used that money to buy cigarette from a nearby store.

This routine followed for some days after which Manasvi revealed the matter to us one night. When I asked him why he didn't tell us this on the first day itself, he said, "I wanted to be sure of what was going around. Had I told you on the first day, a small loss of two hundred rupees might not have affected Tapasvi. But now, since he has been cheated for five days in a row, this lesson will strike him hard."

▼

Around 2008, Tapasvi started using his crutches. Before that, he used to wear those special shoes which were designed to give shape to his feet. They were elephantine and had metal clasps poking out from the sides.

I had always carried Tapasvi everywhere on my back – to the doctor, to his school, on our trips, everywhere.

In 2006 we went to Udaipur. We went to meet Tapasvi's cousin who was pursuing his engineering there. His hostel room was on the third floor. I carried him on the stairs till the third floor on my shoulders. Tapasvi's cousin offered to come to the rest house to meet us, but I just didn't want to deprive Tapasvi of seeing what a hostel looks like. With the passage of time, my physical strength was dwindling as I was getting older. I suffered from a slipped disc five years ago and was in bed for almost a month. That's when Manasvi took more charge and actively performed the role of Tapasvi's elder brother. He handled everything impeccably. My doubts about 'What after me' started to melt away slowly.

Manasvi had matured gracefully. He was aware of his strengths and weaknesses and his command over his languages was incredible. From being a rebellious teenager who threw tantrums at the dining table to a responsible son and brother, Manasvi had come a long way.

Manasvi is very attached to his mother as she has been with him throughout. I was always trying to build the gap that had emerged between both of us. Even after making repeated efforts, I could not solidify our connection.

Manju noticed my struggle. She sat down with me one night, with a cup of coffee, and said, "Manasvi is your child and he will always be. But a lot of time has passed, Ajay. The clock can't be rewinded now. Manasvi is the one who will wear your shoes for Tapasvi's sake when we will not be around anymore. But for now, let him breathe. Accept the fact that you were not around when he needed you. And now, he doesn't need you to be around."

Manasvi is an ardent Shiva follower, maybe that is where his rebellious energy and spiritual self come from. On a trip last year, I wanted to take Tapasvi on my back so that he could savour the sunset from the hill top. But, I was also worried about the fact that I may not be able to endure the burden due to my physical limitations. That's when Manasvi stepped into my shoes, without being asked to do so. He said that he would piggyback Tapasvi.

It was a steep climb, but Manasvi didn't deter. My boys embarked upon their destination, with the orange golden sun casting its rays on them. Their laughter echoing in the vicinity, spreading the affection and commitment they showcased for each other.

▼

Some people might wonder how am I an extraordinary parent? After all, every parent is supposed to nurture their child.

But no one can understand how dependent Tapasvi was on me, even for his basic tasks.

With the passage of time, a child becomes capable enough to take care of himself and be on his own. But Tapasvi would need my assistance. Tapasvi's hands and feet were too firm. They did't work in synchronisation with the whole body. When I tried to help Tapasvi so that he could wear a pant, his feet didn't cooperate and bent. I had to make him swivel his feet and legs first and then make him change his clothes.

This is the kind of meticulous care Tapasvi would always need.

Whenever I thought about the pertinent question, 'What after me' I used to get very worried. I knew that Manju and Manasvi would be there to look after them. Tapasvi was also mushrooming now and had already crossed his teenage. His personal space was violated when I gave him a bath, but both of us knew that there was no other way out. With time, Tapasvi became more comfortable with me.

▼

Tapasvi had come a long way since his childhood days. Now he could perform a lot of tasks on his own, such as fetching the water bottle from the kitchen, switching on the lights and playing the music system.

Due to his unwavering dedication and hard work, Tapasvi was able to clear his NET exam just by listening to audio books.

Since Tapasvi suffers from dyslexia, he could't read books, but his physical and medical condition did not come in the way of his dreams. We were sceptical of him memorising such a protracted syllabus, but he amazed us with his grit and dedication. He not only kept the information in his mind, he also cleared NET with flying colours.

It was through his unwavering resilience that he surmounted about thirty percent of cerebral palsy. We were certain that with two years of persistent physiotherapy, Tapasvi would emerge into a self-reliant individual.

9

Tapasvi's College Experiences

"History was my first love but I was forcefully married to Political Science."

This was Tapasvi's response when someone asked him about his choice of subjects.

Tapasvi faced the same dilemma which every child faces after passing twelfth standard boards – about which field to pursue.

Tapasvi enjoyed studying history. He wanted to pursue his higher education in history and get selected in Indian Foreign Services (IFS). Till now, Tapasvi had studied in Umang, which was a differently-abled student friendly school. But, we were not aware of any such colleges.

While selecting colleges, we had to keep a lot of factors in mind, the primary being the availability of ramps in college premises. Since Tapasvi had studied in an English medium school, we had to shortlist an English medium college.

It is aptly said that history repeats itself.

We had to face a lot of challenges while searching for the best college for Tapasvi. Not all colleges were willing to accept Tapasvi, in spite of his excellent twelfth grade results.

Tapasvi was selected in Delhi University, but we couldn't relocate there as Manasvi was studying in Jaipur. After a frantic search and multiple rejections, we enrolled Tapasvi to Parishkar College in Jaipur for his graduation.

I was very sceptical about Tapasvi going to college all by himself since he had been under our close supervision throughout his school days. A plethora of questions emerged in my mind.

How would Tapasvi handle the environment? How would Tapasvi strike friendship with the other kids? How would other children treat him? How would Tapasvi protect himself if someone bullied him?

The moment Tapasvi took admission in Parishkar College, all my apprehensions melted away. His college environment was very conducive and his peers were very cordial. The used to eat lunch with Tapasvi in the class since he couldn't walk till the canteen. Tapasvi used to share his class notes with the rest of his class too.

We came across a disturbing issue that Tapasvi couldn't fill OMR sheets. They were mandatory as a tool so we bought unused OMR sheets home for Tapasvi to practice. We wanted him to get comfortable with colouring those mini ovals black. Tapasvi was determined to do well in studies. He was so dedicated that he never wasted a single minute of his day. Even when he had nothing to do, he used to sit in lectures he had not opted for. Geography, for instance.

Tapasvi always displayed levels of endurance which I found extraordinary for his age. During his first year exams, he couldn't take one of his exams because of some confusion that I had. He lost out on the exam, but not his composure. He assuaged me saying, "Papa, past is past. What can't be undone shouldn't be thought about. Let's concentrate on tomorrow's exam." These wee-bitty moments constituted his Bachelor's degree days. Tapasvi topped the whole batch by the year-end.

The same question arose after graduation – which university to choose.

Post-graduation in history wasn't available in English medium. Sending him to another city on his own was out of question, so the dilemma arose once again. Finally, we filled entrance exam forms of Rajasthan University and since we had limited options in history, we opted for political science as a subject too.

I discussed Tapasvi's decision of choosing political science with various lecturers, college director and administrative officers. All of them had the same thing to say, "Mr Ajay, do not think twice before getting Tapasvi admitted in political science; it is a subject which will be useful in any competitive examinations he will be appearing in."

When the entrance examination results were declared, I was amazed to see that Tapasvi had scored more in political science than history, but Tapasvi wouldn't have it any other way. He wanted to study history only.

One morning, Tapasvi came to my room and said that he was ready to break up with his love history and marry the subject of my choice 'political science'. I was happy to know that he had changed his mind.

Later I came to know that he had overheard my conversation with my wife one night, regarding what subject should Tapasvi choose. While Tapasvi started going to Rajasthan University for his Master's, we started our search for Tapasvi's home tutor for political science. That's when we met Mr Lalit, the angel in Tapasvi's career.

Lalit worked really hard with Tapasvi as he himself was preparing his lectureship exam in those days. Slowly and gradually, Lalit became the backbone of Tapasvi's education. He taught Tapasvi with so much patience and competence that Tapasvi forgot his first love much sooner than expected.

I was really worried about sending Tapasvi to the university as it was the first time that he was getting exposed to such a big group of students, but Tapasvi made all my worries vanish into thin air. He not only adjusted in the environment, but also carved a niche for himself.

On the one hand, his college was going on; on the other, Lalit was working hard to teach him political science. Lalit was appearing for NET examination and he asked us to fill up Tapasvi's form too. I did not agree with them as I did not believe that he was ready to face the examination. But they went ahead anyway!

For me, it was a dry run exam that Tapasvi was taking. But Lalit was sure about his success. The day of the results came and along with it came the day that was god's reward for my child's twenty-two years of despondency, drudgery, hard work and endurance. Initially I was not inclined towards making Tapasvi appear for the exam. But the day Tapasvi took the exam, I felt a new ray of hope light up within me. I could constantly feel the slight fluttering of hope in my heart after Tapasvi's exam.

On the day of the result, I woke up at 5 a.m. as usual, woke Tapasvi up at 5:30 and followed the same set of rituals. The only thing out of ordinary was having butterflies in my stomach. Contrary to that, Tapasvi was the same serene, poised person. It was like any other run-of-the-mill type of day for him. While I was really sweating bullets about his result, he acted normal, portrayed no emotions, nothing.

At about 10:00, after Tapasvi had finished his breakfast, I couldn't resist the temptation to ask him if he was not having jitters about his result. To that, Tapasvi replied, "Papa, I don't expect anything, ever. Whatever will happen, will happen for good."

I think he wanted to say more, but at that very moment, Tapasvi's mobile screen flashed. There was a message from his best friend asking him to check the results as the results had just been declared. We ran to the computer, and by the time the internet connection could be established, I had cursed almost all and sundry – from the internet service provider for slow connectivity to the government for not reprimanding these service providers.

Those five minutes seemed like five hours to me. Tapasvi had cleared NET, while Lalit cleared the JRF exam. I had tears in my eyes when I saw the results. Those twenty-two years brandished in front of my eyes, moving like a camera roll. I didn't know how to react, weather to be happy or to cry. It was as if all my prayers had been answered, all my dedication and persistence had finally paid off.

My eyes moved from Manju's face to Manasvi's to Tapasvi's report card. I was just not contented, I was excited beyond words. I just didn't know how to praise Lalit, the man behind the show. I felt as if he had become Tapasvi's crutches in education, helping him to move forward, putting one foot after the other, as if acting like a catalyst.

Tapasvi's story is in newspapers today, after his exam results. They are calling it a phenomenal feat by a child suffering from cerebral palsy and dyslexia. A child who cannot write and read because of his impairment has fought all odds to clear this tough exam. The day I envisioned Tapasvi as a lecturer, it seemed a faraway castle in the air. I have had episodes of people making fun of me, terming my endeavour for Tapasvi as a vain effort, but it was those laughs that acted as a stimulus for me to work harder with my kid. I always thought that the day Tapasvi would achieve something in his life, I will go and answer those same people. But the moment I saw the newspaper, I felt as if the reply had already been given by my child. Tapasvi's result is the perfect answer and Tapasvi has answered them himself.

> *"There was always a minority afraid of something, and a great majority afraid of the dark, afraid of the future, afraid of the past, afraid of present, afraid of themselves and shadows of themselves".*
>
> – Ray Bradbury, Fahrenheit 451

Tapasvi is that minority!

10

Crutches – Baggage or Liberation

I always wanted to provide a very safe and nurturing environment for my family, predominantly for Tapasvi.

The biggest impediment that I faced was when no insurance company was ready to offer Tapasvi health or life insurance. Whichever policy I opted for, it came with its own set of terms and conditions.

As per census report of 2011, in India, 26.8 million people are suffering from chronic disabilities. And in India, there are only a few and no government insurance companies which have insurance policies for differently-abled individuals, most of which do not have any comprehensive benefits. A legislation for

Rights for Person with Disabilities Act, (PWD) was passed by the Government in 2016, but like any other Government Act, it was sporadically implemented.

Tapasvi was elated when this act came into force. I knew that it may not be that effective, but I chose to remain silent so as not to dampen his spirits. With time, he realised that such acts are not enforced properly.

Isn't is surprising that till some years back, the Disabled Commissioner's Office of Jaipur didn't have a ramp! The Taj Mahal didn't have ramp ingress! Even McDonald's didn't have a ramp in any of its outlets till a few years ago.

I, along with other parents, had gone with the staff of Umang and remonstrated in front of McDonald's holding placards that stated that "Mc Donald's bought their burgers to India but forgot their ramps."

When the ramp was belatedly built outside the Rajmandir outlet of McDonald's, all the students of Umang were taken for a treat by the school authorities there. It was for the first time that Tapasvi went out with his friends.

We have a whole lot of government jobs in India with reservation policy attached to it. As stated in the Constitution of India, reservation is generally given to weaker sections of the society, then why don't we have reservation for differently-abled children?

They are also a marginalized section of the society. I believe that especially in jobs related to the education sector, such as lectureship they should be given reservation so that they can lead a meaningful life.

The Government of India provides pension for persons with disabilities, but there are no slabs in it. It is undeniable that a person with twenty percent disability needs less financial assistance than a person with eighty percent disability. Also, the financial background of the family should be considered. Have you even seen a Member of Local Assembly (MLA) or Member of Parliament (MP) who is disabled? Have you ever seen a minister who is even twenty percent disabled? None! Disabled people have no representation in the Government of India.

There isn't a single NGO in India that has been instituted for differently-abled kids by someone other than the parents of effected kids. There are no skill centres for these kids and there are no government employment centres for people belonging to the so-called 'disabled' category. There is no security service for children with challenges, for that matter. What if the parents of these children are handling them insensitively? A child with cognitive abilities can find his escape route in such circumstances, but what about the specially-abled ones?

There are many instances where differently-abled children – especially females – have been subjected to physical exploitation by relatives or close family members. If we look at less-fortunate sections of the society, drinking and then physically exploiting the disabled girls is a common occurrence. There is hardly any institution or agency to raise their voice against such atrocities, barring the women empowerment activists in some cases.

In such situations, even mothers cannot step out and complain about family members exploiting their daughters with special needs to safeguard their family name and the child's social reputation. I once met a mother whose daughter was admitted to a hospital after her father molested her, and then beat her up so that she doesn't detail this matter to anybody. During the discussion, that lady was inconsolable and told me, "Sahab, we are poor people. This has been going on since the last two years, but I didn't report the matter to the police. Nobody will marry my incapacitated daughter and if her father throws her out of the house, where will we go? Nobody will give us food. We will starve. Her father is exploiting her within the four walls of the house, but the moment we step out of those walls, others will do that too."

I was aghast beyond words. I just didn't know what could soothe her pain and make her aware enough to speak up.

I am indebted to god that he made me capable enough to fulfil all the needs of Tapasvi. Money, for that matter, was never a matter of concern. This was one of the reasons why both, Manju and I, retained our jobs and managed alongside, as we had to keep the cash flow for Tapasvi's treatment. But what about those who can't afford such treatments? Most of the accessories and operations are really costly. No bank loans are granted to parents for treatment. Also, there are no specific child care leaves for parents in such cases. No day-care facilities are seen for specially-abled children too. People are not mentally strong and prepared enough to walk that extra mile to serve this particular section of society. There is no other person to take care of a special child, except the parents. But of course, I feel staunchly about the subject because Tapasvi is my son. If it would have been anybody else's child, I wouldn't have been advocating this subject. But now, since I have the issue hitting me personally, I have iron-jawed to fight for the rights of these children.

I even filed a PIL regarding the same in court. I understand that the battle would not be easy.

I have a blueprint about curtain-raising a respite care facility for parents with differently-abled kids. Parents miss out on their lives; I have missed out on mine. I have missed attending any functions and gatherings because leaving my child alone at home was never a prerogative. As a result, I could never fulfil my social obligations. I paint really well, but now I don't even know in which corner of the house my brushes and canvas lie. I play chess really well, but now I have started getting befuddled between planning a move of rook and bishop. When I last played badminton, I can't even recollect the year. My wife never attends kitties, doesn't go out with her friends. She doesn't have the luxury of her 'me' time. We don't have a big friends' circle, except for my seven friends. Similarly, Tapasvi also gets piqued many a times, when he isn't able to carry family obligations or handle family matters; it pinches him. He never says anything, but we both know the facts. With each passing day, as he is mushrooming, his perspective of standpoint and people is changing.

It was midnight when my father expired, both my kids were sleeping in the same room. I rushed to the hospital the moment I got a call from the emergency wing, it was 2:30 a.m. of April 2019, to be precise. I didn't wake up my kids, didn't tell them anything before leaving for the hospital. The next morning when my fathers' body was bought to the house, Manasvi had a lot to do; he had a lot of chores to perform. Tapasvi didn't have any role to play, even if I wanted to give him any amenability, I just couldn't figure out which onus to assign him. It was a haphazard situation. I had just lost my father and on the other hand, I didn't have a second to spare for Tapasvi in the germinal few days after the demise. I didn't even let my tears spill in front of Tapasvi and Tapasvi, in fine feather that he always has been, didn't shed a tear in front of me. Later, my house help told me that when we all went to the cremation ground, Tapasvi closed the door of his room and the wailing could be heard till the balcony.

While we were going to the cremation ground, Tapasvi asked to be escorted along, which was not a viable proposal in that state of affairs. With a heavy heart, we had to spurn Tapasvi. My elder brother told Tapasvi that he will have to stay at home as an emotionally strong man has to remain back to take care of the female clan. Both Tapasvi and my brother knew it was a palter, but my brother put a serious face in front of Tapasvi and Tapasvi accepted as if whatever reason my brother was explaining was legitimate. Both didn't have the luxury of a second option.

Tapasvi feels bad or rather culpable many a times about me and my wife not being able to have a chipper, blooming social life because of him. He has pointed out this matter to me and that is factual to an extent. But I wouldn't want it any other way, ever.

"Dear life, you are exhausting at times. You throw more tantrums than I have ever known possible. You slow down, you speed up, you take time and give time. Sometimes there is sunshine and other times there are storms. So I try to break it up a little, take risks, love a lot, and find comfort in trying new things. But you are never the same, life. Always changing, always keep me guessing. So I will live you, life, to my absolute potential."

11

Embracing the Difference

It was already dusk by the time Mr Sharma had a glass of water which was lovingly given by his wife.

"She knows me the most. Twenty-four years is not a short span of time," he says.

"You voice was quivering. I could sense that you were emotional," she replied. Her smile was pleasant and serene.

By that time, Tapasvi had entered the room again. He was not escorted by anybody but his crutches.

"I am going to meet my friends. And since it is a celebration of my result, the treat is on me. Papa, could you please drop me to the café and also give me some money?" he asked with a smile.

Mr Ajay asked his wife to keep my company while he went out of the drawing room. Mrs Manju came to interact with me. Her eyes were brimming with courage and grit.

"You see," she spoke, "when we got married on 8 February 1996, little did we know that life would be so unpredictable for us. Ajay has been a caring husband always. I feel so blessed to have him in my life. I couldn't have asked for more."

"Sometimes, I wonder if I have consciously named my boy, 'Tapasvi', the one who does Tapasya, austerity. If his life had been so strenuous because of his name! There are certain negative thoughts which invade my mind very often. But then, Ajay keeps me going when the times are tough. I have held Ajay tight, in my arms and in my heart."

By the time our conversation came to an end, Tapasvi entered the drawing room. He was looking smart. We reached the parking area of the house and Tapasvi got into the car with the help of his father. I hopped in as well as I had to go to the airport.

On the way to café, Tapasvi talked about his friends with an air of exhilaration. Megha, Vidhya, Karan, Puru, Eshan and Lokesh. They were his best mates since Umang days, with whom he could discuss almost everything. Most of them were just like him – special children who were enjoying their lives.

By the time we reached the café, all his friends had reached there.

"Tapasvi, always the late comer! Congratulations bro!" one of them remarked. The other one patted Tapasvi on the back while one of the girls pulled out a gift from her bag. I was touched by their affectionate bond.

As we went to the car, Mr Ajay told me, “Have you ever seen a bumblebee? The aerodynamic law isn’t applicable on it. The bee cannot fly because the wings are small in comparison to the weight of the bee. But it flies courageously. Tapasvi is my bumblebee.”

I looked in the direction of the café. I could see Tapasvi laughing with his friends. The sunlight glistened on the glass window, making the surroundings look more golden. As it created an aura of orange all around Tapasvi, it looked like the fighter, the survivor had been amply rewarded. In the backdrop I could see a bougainvillea plant, the flowerets turned to a rosy colour in the dusky sun, casting a shadow on the opposite walls of the café.

A meeting was held quite far from earth,
It's time again for another birth,
Said the angels to the Lord above,
This special child will need much love.

His progress may be very slow,
Accomplishments he may not show,
And he'll require extra care,
From the folks he meets down there.

He may not run or laugh or play,
His thoughts may seem quite far away,
In many ways he won't adapt,
And he'll be known as handicapped.

So let's be careful where he's sent,
We want his life to be content,
Please Lord, find the parents who,
Will do a special job for you.

They will not realise right away,
The leading role they are asked to play,
But with this child sent from above,
Comes stronger faith and richer love.

And soon they'll know the privilege given,
In caring for their gift from Heaven,
Their precious charge, so meek and mild,
Is HEAVEN'S VERY SPECIAL CHILD.

– Edna Massimilla

Epilogue

In Tapasvi's Words

"I am like a painting created by various artists. People and their influences have coloured it in hues and shades of tangerine, amber and maroon."

I want my father to have some life for himself, but he doesn't even know that he is devoid of it. His life revolves around me, which overwhelms sometimes, but most of the time, it acts as an inspiration for me. I always wondered if he had some regrets about whatever he did for me as he clearly worked very hard to support my well-being.

I don't treasure much of my childhood. Most of it was filled with stinging realisations. I was never a child who would play around with my toys. Rather, I was the child who saw his younger brother play and run around.

I was the child who banged his head on the floor because he couldn't play. I was the child who was bullied. Once at lunch, my classmates challenged me to go into a cage. And just to prove to them that I could do it, I reluctantly walked into it. To ridicule me even more, they locked me up and jeered about how they'd even leave some rats in it.

When the teacher found me, she scolded me for coming out of the classroom. That incident intensified my fear. Since that day, I realized that the only way I could attain a life of respect and dignity was by working hard and excelling in my studies. My education is the only way through which I can build myself and refine my life. This was the only way through which I was able to change the perception about people like me.

I couldn't share the humiliation I faced at school with my father because I know how concerned he would become if he got to know about my plight. Any parent would!

I was the child who woke up every morning and saw his family going around doing things independently while I could not even move. They didn't need anyone to help them for basic tasks like putting on their slippers or drinking water. I would often drown in self pity as I was unaware of who I was. But, there were defining episodes which acted as milestones to make me realize how special I was. To be different was actually very empowering!

Once, my father left me standing near a wall. He particularly asked me not to move. But I didn't stand still. When has a child followed all the commands diligently?

I fell on my face. As I lay on the ground, I couldn't get up. When my dad found me, everyone was startled. I had a faint idea that something was wrong with me, but that awareness was yet to sink in.

Another episode which made me realize that I was different was when my mother took me to a bank. On my way, I saw a few kids playing cricket. I was fascinated and wanted to play too.

I asked my mother to take me to the playground. She agreed to my request but sensed that I was disheartened. There was no way in which I could bat, field or run for scores.

To uplift my spirits, my mother said, "Don't worry, Tapasvi! When you will become old and move to a higher class, you will be able to play with them."

Every time I asked her if I was old enough to go out and play, she would add another year. My day never really came. I knew that she was sad because I was bereft of the joys of playing freely with other kids. To fulfil my wish, she even tried to hold me and made me grip the bat and hit the ball. But it didn't really work.

However, instead of being discouraged, I decided to play on my strengths. I knew I may not be able to get the field experience, but no one can stop me from expanding my knowledge about this subject. I decided to read everything about the sport. Watching legends like Saurav Ganguly and Rahul Dravid also played a huge part in broadening my horizons.

There was one more incident that changed my life. It was the time when I was sitting with my legs in a W position and my father pushed me in anger.

There are a lot of things I don't tell my father. Like, how much I detested getting Botox. My three months were wasted as I couldn't study or sleep. All I did was exercise. How would you feel if you wake up after an operation and find yourself in chains?

I was stretched, tautened like an elastic band for twenty hours a day for three months. There was nothing I could do about it.

Sometimes I feel my father was too strict as a coach. He took me to a park once and told me that he won't pick me up if I fall. It made me apprehensive as I was not ready for this. It made me realise that my father won't always be around to support me. There would be a time when I would be on my own. This constant dependence on others often make me think.

What's the point of my education if I keep cumbering the life of my family members?

When a child is born, the happiest person undoubtedly is the mother. As they say, "Behind every successful man is a woman." Similarly, I believe that behind every successful son, there is a loving mother's endearment and sacrifices. My mother is a strong and courageous woman who has supported me through everything. In my initial days, when I felt that exercises were not helping me, she patiently explained the benefits of physiotherapy, filling me with enthusiasm and hope every time. She was always there to motivate me and my father, acting as our pillar of strength.

At the time of Botox, I was advised rigorous exercises. One day, while I was sleeping in the afternoon and there was little time left for my physiotherapy session, my mother received a call from my father. He asked her to trim me properly for my physiotherapy session as it was a regular feature at the time of Botox.

I overheard her saying, "Please let Tapasvi sleep peacefully. He is our child, not a machine."

She held me tight and said, "I know Tapasvi, every morning when you get up, you are uncertain about which road to take. Most of the time, your path is full of hurdles. But son, believe me, we will have to continue our journey like this anyway and we will do it together."

▼

I am an atheist. People have a tendency to believe in superficial manifestations of religion. But for me, the essence of god doesn't lie in *diyas* or idols. Rather, it is the spirit of giving which inspires us to support the unprivileged and impoverished to create a more harmonious society.

I witnessed the death of people. One was a close friend who also happened to be a talented painter. He was a brilliant student, but unfortunately, his family couldn't save him. He used to stay locked up in his house and eventually, he gave up.

Whenever I think about his plight, it fills my heart with sorrow. I will never get over the injustice that people with disabilities face. I wish everyone could get a father like mine, perhaps a little less stringent!

The second death was the death of my dear grandfather. He loved me immensely. When I had chicken pox, I was feeling spiritless and wanted to watch TV. He immediately called the cable guy so that my wish could be fulfilled.

Once he asked me if I wanted a camera so that I could preserve the beautiful memories of my life. That gesture made me feel very special.

When my grandfather fell and broke his hip bone, he was taken to the hospital. Before going, he told me that he won't be coming back. When he didn't come back after a long time, I knew something was very wrong.

I wanted to go and meet him in the hospital, but my father didn't permit me to go there. He said that my grandfather had lost his memory and doesn't recall anything, that he probably won't recognize me either. While everyone else went to meet him, it was only me who wasn't taken to the hospital.

Then, one night, my father got a call from the hospital, telling him that my grandfather had passed away. While everyone went to the hospital, I woke my brother and broke the news to him. I felt very helpless at that moment. I couldn't do anything other than informing all the relatives about the death. When everyone was in the hospital or busy pulling things together for the funeral, I got up and went to the little temple that we have in our house. I wanted to pick up the idol and crush it, but couldn't muster the strength to do so. My eyes were brimming with tears as I knew that it was going to be an irreparable loss.

When everyone went to the pyre, I was left abaft. I stayed back and held my grandmother for a long time. But after a while, my mother asked me to go and rest. I was already despondent of the fact that I was not able to help my family and this statement added fuel to the fire. I was aching and bewailing.

I felt so remorseful for not being able to serve and help my grandfather in his last moments. There would always be situations and circumstances where my physical limitation would hinder me from making a considerable difference to improve the situation. And the worst part was that I couldn't even prevent myself from allowing negative thoughts to overwhelm my mind.

There are so many people who are putting in so much efforts so that I can have a better life. My life is a product of a series of sacrifices made by my family and friends to ensure my happiness. Instead of letting this thought bring me down, I use it to strengthen my self confidence.

I don't have any other option but to succeed. I have always strived to focus and do well in my studies. Reading books is like meditation to me.

Once, during one of my exams, a writer cancelled at the last moment due to some unexpected circumstances. My father had to beg a twelfth standard girl so that she could agree to become my writer. I remember that scene vividly. My father was folding his hands to convince the girl to help me so that I don't lose out on my studies. And, I couldn't do anything other than watching from behind the curtain.

I know I should be grateful to every single person who has supported me in my journey, but is it fair for them to help me by keeping their own comfort and happiness at stake? How can I ever evaluate myself if I am using the help of writers?

From day one, I had a choice. Either I could let myself drown in self-pity or I could take my father's hand and carve my path towards a bright future. I never thought that I won't have a good life because my father was always there for me. It is his faith and conviction that has made me into the person that I am today.

Once, I was sitting in my room when my father entered. He put his hand on my shoulder and said, "Tapasvi! I want you to be independent."

I felt extremely happy to know that my family considered me worthy enough to give me responsibilities. It was a very gratifying moment, but my war isn't over yet.

I want my father to not worry about me so much. I want my brother to live a happy life without sacrificing his dream. I want to become an inspiration for others. My physical condition is not a disability; rather, it is my ability to do different and extraordinary things.

This sun that you see every day, it shines with its own light. Apart from rising magnificently, it spreads its light benevolently and illuminates the rest of the world. The moon graciously borrows its light from the sun and glows with its own might.

My father has always been the sun of my life. And, I am the moon. I always hope to learn, evolve and grow under his nurturing care.

Sadhvi Sharma
Education Department, Delhi

Ajay's life changed significantly when Tapasvi came into his life. He is the reason that made him 'the Ajay' that is being written about today. Until Tapasvi came into the picture, Ajay used to be a regular guy who was leading a conventional life. With the advent of Tapasvi, what changed?

The 'boy' became a 'man'. When he got married, I saw him as an admiring husband who would take care of his wife, who would stand by her in her decisions, and most importantly, who would never forget his wife's birthdays or anniversaries and that is how life moved on for this couple.

Then, one rainy July night, he became a father. Fatherhood brings in many major changes in a man's life too. The irresponsible husbands transform into mature and responsible fathers almost suddenly. In Ajay's life, it was a double bonanza as they were blessed with twins. It was exciting yet exhausting as life started moving at a rapid pace. Among the twins, while one would sleep, the other would cry. If one was peacefully having milk, the other one threw up his share!

It took some time to realize that Ajay was chosen by god to have a special kid who made him a special father in years to come.

He had patience, but we never knew it was this much!

He had dedication that was never explored!

He had zeal, but it was never measured!

He had hope, but that became the epitome of confidence!

Tapasvi made him a different person, transforming him for good. After Tapasvi's diagnosis, life did not remain the same for the family. Tapasvi's mother became a woman who worked incredibly hard, perhaps more than everybody else. Her mornings would start too early, but she took it in her stride.

Tapasvi's twin became a less demanding baby. All parents try to do their best for their children, but parents of a special child become special too, as they walk an extra mile. God has expressed his faith in the family, knowing that with them, this child would reach the potential he is bestowed with. I am pleased to be a part of this extended family.

Ever since Manasvi and Tapasvi blessed Ajay's family, their days stretched and night became shorter. After Tapasvi's diagnosis, Ajay took it upon himself to co-conceive the dreams with him and work towards achieving them. They both started taking steps together to conquer the world. After his work, Ajay was always thrilled to spend his time with Tapasvi. He would drive straight for home to be with Tapasvi, to give attention to Tapasvi's daily exercises and tending to his physiotherapy.

A man can live so many lives; we all do play different roles in our lives. Each role is demanding. One has to prioritize and decide which role to play as a lead and which one to keep as dormant.

Ajay chose to play a very special role; he played the lead in the capacity of a special father for a special child.

▼

Taruna Gupta
Government Lecturer, Chandigarh
(Ajay's Batchmate)

The year was 2009 and it was that time of the year when sultry summers were still ahead and there was some spring left in the air. We had planned a trip to Jaipur and Udaipur after our elder son's matriculation examination. The idea rang a bell somewhere in my mind and I called up Ajay, an old college friend settled in Jaipur.

He greeted me warmly. And upon reaching Jaipur, it became our routine to call him in the morning. He would chalk out the day for us – decide what places to visit, what routes to take and which food joints to try.

On the third day of our stay, it was his birthday. So he gave us a choice for second half of the day – either a visit to Chokhi Dhani, a famous ethnic resort, or spending the evening at his place. I smilingly told him that there was no question of choice and we would love to celebrate his birthday at home with the entire family. And how right we were!

The evening unfolded beautifully and became the most memorable one for us. Our families were meeting for the first time. I saw aunty after a long time.

That day, we enjoyed the most delectable Rajasthani food most lovingly prepared and most endearingly served. I could feel the long hours of affectionate labour put in the kitchen by Manju, Ajay's wife. The house was filled with the laughter of children and the sounds of chit chat, Manju and I savouring food together and aunty indulging us.

However, there was more to the evening that etched it in my memory. It was then that I met Tapasvi for the first time. We found him to be a vivacious child with a smiling face, talking confidently and zestfully, full of anecdotes and interesting facts. Later, my kids would often refer to facts and jokes shared by Tapasvi. But more than these, what touched me was the empathy and love in his eyes.

Ajay and I had not been in regular touch with each other so I did not know much about Tapasvi, except that he suffered from some physical impairment. It was only after our visit to Jaipur that we got to know the extent of his problems. We could see that it had been a battle on many fronts for the family as well – to nurture the child to his full potential, to make arrangements for his treatment, therapies, training and education, to give him a fulfilling and quality life.

Acceptance of oneself should first come from within before one expects to be accepted by others. For Tapsavi, it was imperative to have enough confidence to accept himself as a dignified person. We live in a society which has little awareness and even lesser empathy for children with special needs. In this scenario, it was an incredible task to make Tapasvi a part of the mainstream and fulfil his social and educational needs and aspirations.

It is because of their indomitable will, undeterred endeavour and perseverance that they were able to succeed, despite multiple setbacks and hindrances due to lack of adequate facilities like proper rehabilitation centres, educational institutes, trained teachers and educators. Tapasvi has done exceedingly well in his academics. I remember Ajay calling and telling me in a voice filled with excitement that Tapasvi had qualified NET in his very first attempt.

Ajay has made Tapasvi his tapas, his mission in life. He is a role model for parents. And so is Manju. Ajay could fully devote himself to the care of Tapasvi only because Manju did not burden him with the concerns of household drudgery, social responsibilities and commitments, including upbringing of Manasvi. Both of them have complemented each other. It is their joint effort as a family in which Manasvi, their parents and other family members have had their own share of responsibilities, duties and sacrifices.

Everyone around Tapasvi needed to reconstruct, restructure, mould and modify their life in accordance with Tapasvi's needs and requirements. Tapasvi made of a part of their heart and soul, their dreams and desires, and in short, their whole being. It has been a long, laborious and difficult journey of challenges, hardships, rejections, disappointments and failures.

At the same time, it is also an inspirational saga of never giving up, celebrating little joys and successes, living life to its fullest and emerging victorious. Here is a fine example of what human endeavour, courage, grit and resoluteness are capable of accomplishing in spite of mammoth impediments and barriers.

It is not easy to be Tapasvi. It is also not easy to be Ajay. May they continue their journey and explore new horizons together.

▼

H S Nandwana
Deputy Secretary, Law
Jaipur

Ajay and I have been colleagues since 1994, though not very close. Like others, he was one of my batch-mates and I could not see his inner qualities which might impress me, before he became a father. I remember of ridiculing him once for purchasing a car model which was not very fascinating. It was then that Ajay, for first time, explained the situation to me. He had deliberately purchased that model as it had a high ceiling which facilitated him to enter inside with his kid, Tapasvi who used to sit on his lap. This arrangement would save him from bumping against the ceiling of the car. Ultimately, I came to know that one of his twins is suffering from cerebral palsy.

Ajay named his kid Tapasvi. It seems that he had been aware of the fate that his son would have to undergo. The day a child is born, everything changes in a man's life. A man no longer remains the same person who is ready to take risks. He is no longer the carefree person like before.

Ajay had always been serious in discharging his professional duties as well as those for his sons. He never left any scope because of which his specially challenged kid may infer that he is not given importance or is being ignored.

Ajay did signify the proverb 'Good fathers make good sons'. It is the encouragement by his father which made Tapasvi a man of substance. Today, Tapasvi is a NET qualified scholar. A great dad always supports his son. Ajay, undoubtedly, is a great father.

Many a time, I have seen him in pain due to his slip disc. It happened because he stretched his arm to open the water tap which was a little away from his reach. Ajay did not want to disturb his son Tapasvi who was enjoying his bath, sitting in his father's lap.

What Barack Obama said about a father squarely fits on Ajay. It is the courage to raise a child that makes you a father. I can reiterate the saying that the quality of a father can be seen in the goals, dreams and aspirations he sets not only for himself, but for his family.

The bond between Ajay and Tapasvi has also made me sensitive towards persons with benchmark disabilities. Keeping in mind the dedication and constant efforts of Ajay for bringing up Tapasvi, I can say that Pam Brown truly observed that 'Dads are most ordinary men turned into heroes'. Ajay too, is a hero. As my friend's name connotes a man who cannot be conquered. Ajay is invincible.

▼

Neeraj Sharma
Public Prosecutor, Ada
Haryana Government

Ajay and I have known each other since 1983, around thirty-eight years. I am always sceptical while using the term 'know each other' because, a person may not know him/herself even after completion of journey of life. Still, in our case, it would be appropriate to say that we know each other. Ajay is blessed with certain qualities – Conviction towards your beliefs, courage to speak and follow your principles, and most importantly, to never give up. These qualities coupled with your fighting spirit are the root and soul of his relationship with Tapasvi.

Nature has blessed living creatures with emotions – some positive and some negative. Love and affection with kids being the most important one among them. We perceive our kids as our own extension. Is Ajay's relationship with Tapasvi a result of that common emotion in every father? My reply without any hesitation would be a clear 'NO'.

Ajay's spirit to figure it out and fight it out has given new meaning to the emotional values and strings with which both the father and son are tied. Ajay is the youngest son among his brothers, but his parents have always stayed with him. Maybe because they could see him as special before us all. If the parents can have this feeling, there is no need to elaborate on how secure Tapasvi must be finding himself under Ajay's wings. Thus, emotion coupled with sense of security is the recipe of Ajay's relationship with Tapasvi.

There was a time when Ajay took the situation as a challenge, which he had to fight. Resultantly, Ajay took charge of Tapasvi as if he was only Ajay's responsibility. I have both seen and perceived Ajay making efforts to improve Tapasvi's physical and emotional strength.

In fact, Ajay has lived Tapasvi's life more than his own. Both of them are like the forces pushing each other to achieve what a common boy can only dream of.

Therefore, it is a dynamic relationship filled with emotional force. We all have our strengths and weaknesses. What is important is to manage the weakness, harp on strengths and move on and this is what both of them are doing.

I would be honest to admit, had I been at Ajay's place, I could not have done things the way Ajay has done and will continue to do. I wish all the best to this wonderful father and son duo.

▼

S L Malik
Retd. Dy. Secretary
Secretariat, Jaipur

I feel really grateful for getting an opportunity to write a few lines about my dear friend Ajay and his son. Although the bond of a father and son is a common affair, but here, the case is different.

Ajay was bestowed with twins and while it bought double the happiness, it also bought with it double the efforts and responsibilities. Overall, it is a difficult task and the difficulty level increases when one of the children is suffering from a prolonged disease.

I came in contact with Ajay when he joined the state government, and luckily, he was posted in my section only. Initially I wasn't aware about his official and family circumstances. I just knew that his wife was also working in the education department and I often used to wonder how tough it must be for him to manage with his twins with both him and his wife working.

By then, I didn't know about Tapasvi's diagnosis. When I came to know about his child's physical limitations and the way he was handling the situation, my respect for him increased manifold. He not only paid his complete attention towards the development of Tapasvi, but also tried to provide him with the best medical facilities available.

I have seen Ajay being very restless and puzzled sometime in office and initially used to wonder why. Later, I realised that it was not restlessness but Ajay's quest to provide the best medical care and physiotherapy for Tapasvi.

Ajay never took his son to be less than anybody and tried to get Tapasvi admitted in regular schools. But, when the process of admission started, the bitter truth between advertisement of so-called hi-fi, reputed schools and their reality was revealed.

Not a single school had such a provision for admission of differently-abled kids. Their common reason used to be inadequate infrastructure, even after advertising about providing these facilities in the newspapers.

Tapasvi also had a big problem with writing as his upper limbs were not worked upon much. During one of our office lunch sessions, Ajay once told me that not a single physiotherapist he has worked with suggested him to work on the upper limbs. Everybody's focus was on the lower limbs and therefore Ajay too concentrated upon physiotherapy on the lower part of the body only, something which he deeply regrets now.

Tapasvi's brain is very sharp, which even I have felt at many instances, but he needs a writer every time he sits for an examination. The brain development and vast expanse of general knowledge of Tapasvi was only possible because of the hard work that Ajay and his family put into it. Ajay not only arranged for the best tutors, but also provides the best writers for Tapasvi. Such writers are not an easy task to find. Ajay's sincere efforts, inspiration and motivation led Tapasvi to qualify all the major examinations that he appeared in. Tapasvi also gave the National Olympiad examination and got success in it.

In the tough and turbulent tide they have sailed in, Ajay has always been the anchor of his ship. Undoubtedly, the father and son are not just a perfect example of bonding, but a motivation for many.

I hope and wish that these tests of life direct towards the bright future of both and they enlighten the path for many to follow.

▼

Shikha Jacob Sharma
Section Officer Law
Secretariat, Jaipur

The woods are lovely dark and deep,
But I have promises to keep,
And miles to go before I sleep,
And miles to go before I sleep.

These are my favourite lines from a Robert Frost poem, and go so well with Ajay, the father of this wonderfully blessed child Tapasvi.

The father I'm talking about is no less than a blessing to his son. You will come to know more as you read this. You may call a part of this biography of a father-son relationship. This became apparent when I heard this from Ajay sir that his son Tapasvi cleared his NET examination and the glow that flashed on his face at that time is beyond any explanation.

I was equally happy because although I have not been a part of his journey, to some extent, I could feel the way he would have felt at that moment.

Once when out of curiosity, I asked Ajay sir how he was managing with this situation, he said with a very bright smile, "Yes, the situation is tough. Sometimes things don't work out the way they should, but once you accept the situation as it is, half of the problem is solved and then you get this incredible energy of facing all the pros and cons of the situation with a positive attitude."

I have seen Ajay sir follow the motto – Never Give Up. I feel really blessed to have met him, as apart from our daily monotonous official work, he used to take out some time to talk with his juniors and his favourite topic of discussion was undoubtedly his beloved son Tapasvi.

Initially I could not relate to him on this topic because even after being a psychology student, I failed to gather his inner-most feelings and couldn't read what all he was going through in his mind while he talked about Tapasvi. But I know for sure that I haven't come across such a father who was so obsessed with helping his son out of this helpless situation that had apparently no solution to it.

It was not easy for him. Being a human being, he felt low and depressed several times, but he often found different ways to cheer himself up and bounce back strongly to face the never-ending struggle.

I am not a staunchly religious person, yet I do believe in the existence of god. We all have heard this famous saying, God cannot be everywhere so he created mothers to take care of every child on this earth.

Here, I could see god in the face of a father of this blessed child who was already crossing mountains to make his child physically and mentally independent. When it comes to mental health, the main thing that matters is how the concerned person who is undergoing such a disorder perceives himself in a society that is full of competition, where everybody is running their own race, having no time to even give a helping hand to someone who needs it.

As far as I can understand, such special persons are vulnerable and often feel that they are incapable. Moreover, they feel detached from the society and fail to gel with the others.

In this case, I saw Ajay clear about his goals concerning Tapasvi. He worked really hard from his physical therapies to his mental strength. He left no stone unturned in building up the mental strength of his son. He ensured Tapasvi never felt he was less than others and in no situation should he feel that he could not fulfil his son's dreams because of the physical hindrances.

Somewhere, Tapasvi also knew that he was not all by himself in this challenging journey. He had full faith in his father who was full of hopes and possibilities, and moreover, he was ready to do anything to help him fulfil his dreams.

Ajay sir is an individual you rarely meet; filled with positivity, hope, possibilities and there is no space for negative thoughts in his life. This is what Tapasvi has inherited from him. This attitude has led him to multiple achievements and given his father a chance to be proud of him.

Being a woman, I know what has to be faced by a working lady, managing home stuff, relationship responsibilities along with the official responsibilities. But as I came to know about this father who, apart from keeping pace with his service responsibilities, was also fulfilling his responsibility towards his differently-abled child, I was deeply inspired.

There is something magical about the father-son relationship, which is hard to find. It's a social set up in our country that mothers are basically responsible for the upbringing of children whereas fathers are busy making money for the family. Either they do not take any interest in the upbringing of children or do not have enough time to spare for them. But Ajay sir turned the dynamics completely.

Subsequently, I came to know about Tapasvi's medical condition, in which an individual has to be dependent upon wheelchair for his movements or on other individuals for little things like brushing, etc.

To my amazement, I saw that this father never wanted his child to be dependent on a wheelchair. He constantly insisted and encouraged him to walk on crutches despite all his discomfort, despite the hard work it involved. I asked him the reason for this and I was touched by his answer. He said, "Walking is a must for effective working of the vital organs, sitting on a wheelchair all the time will lead to indigestion, low lung functioning, less exposure to the sun which is a very important part of our healthy living. Insisting Tapasvi to walk on crutches will not only help improve his metabolism, but also improve his lung functioning and he will be able to breathe normally."

Tapasvi is an intelligent child and he has proved it by clearing the NET exam. This healthy and wide approach of his father towards his son has helped him a lot to achieve this accolade.

I would also like to add further that Ajay sir has laid stressed on the wide social exposure of Tapasvi by choosing a university where he could easily relate with other fellow mates by sharing his thoughts with them and therefore could improve his self-confidence by not feeling any less than others.

Tapasvi's education has been through NGOs. His father had to walk extra miles for his well-being. The reason being, he did not want Tapasvi to feel less than others, feel incompetent. The result was that Tapasvi did not hesitate in moving forward in his life in any field.

Be it academics or creative fields, Ajay sir left no stone unturned to help him feel independent and confident. There used to be an emergency situation in the house whenever Tapasvi took part in any debate, extempore or dance programs. All the family members used to encourage Tapasvi so that he could perform well. Moreover, his father approached famous dancer Shiamak Davar to keep his son high-spirited.

I feel that Tapasvi's father could have chosen an easier way of escaping from his responsibilities, but instead, Ajay sir crossed all the barriers to help his child fulfil all his dreams.

Whenever you talk to Ajay sir, he will talk only about his son Tapasvi and try to figure out what else can he do to make his son independent.

I would like to share a part of our conversation and I was really touched by his thoughts. He said, "Everyone asks what the nation is giving to them, but no one thinks what contribution they are giving to the nation. I want my son Tapasvi to contribute economically or in any way towards the nation and so I have arranged for him assets for his future so that even he can contribute towards the nation like you and I do."

Now this is not what you will hear from every other person, especially not from the father of a differently-abled child. This zeal and purity of thought is what Tapasvi has inherited from his father.

Ajay sir is indeed a god figure to his son. Every day, he wakes up with the hope that he will do his best to strengthen his son both physically and mentally. Maybe, one day, medical sciences could do wonders and invent a solution to this medical condition and at that time, his son will be prepared to accept that solution and improve his life even if his father is not there.

This is a story of a great father whose life revolves around his son with a dream that his efforts may not leave his son vulnerable and not let him *become dependent on his sibling or wife, thereby hindering their natural day to day life, even when he is not in this world.*

Never quit because you never know when you could change the life of your special child and give him a proud life, just like Ajay sir has done for Tapasvi.

List of Acronyms

ADHD	–	Attentive Deficit Hyperactivity Disorder
AFO	–	Ankle and Foot Orthosis
CDC	–	Centers for Disease Control and Prevention
CP	–	Cerebral Palsy
IFS	–	Indian Foreign Services
MP	–	Member of Parliament
MR	–	Mental Retardation
NET	–	National Eligibility Test
NIH	–	National Institutes of Health
NIOS	–	National Institute of Open Learning
SCARED	–	Screen for Child Anxiety Related Emotional Disorders
SDR	–	Selective Dorsal Rhizotomy
SPECT	–	Single-photon Emission Computerized Tomography

Recommended Reading

BECAUSE LIFE IS A GIFT

Disha

The real-life success stories of fifteen differently-abled people charted in this book will make you believe that nothing is impossible if you set your heart on it. You will sense pride replace all feelings of pity and sympathy for they have fought against all odds to achieve their dreams.

This book is a tribute to their courage, passion and zest for life.

ISBN: 978-9382665250; Pages: 208; Format: Paperback; Price: INR 175

A LOVE SO SPECIAL

Deepak Srivastava

Nikhil and Neha have struggled immensely for a good future. When their specially-abled son Raghu goes missing, Nikhil takes it upon himself to find him. He will turn the world upside down if he has to.

The journey takes him back to his roots and a past he has been running from, to prove that a parent will do anything for their child.

ISBN: 978-8194790808; Pages: 200; Format: Paperback; Price: INR 250

MY FATHER IS A HERO

Nishant Kaushik

When the ten-year-old Nisha mysteriously starts spiralling into despair and seclusion, Vaibhav faces the toughest test of his life as a single father – to reclaim his child's trust and happiness. What distance will a middle-class man with limited means go to show his daughter the merit in believing in a dream? Read this gripping tale of love, courage, and of the emergence of an ordinary man as an extraordinary hero.

ISBN: 978-9382665601; Pages: 208; Format: Paperback; Price: INR 195